How to Hit the Second Shot
FIRST

BLUE AND BAWDY JOKES
THAT UNLOCK THE
PUZZLE OF THE GREEN

Jim Bronner & Bob Gilhooley

WARNER BOOKS

NEW YORK   BOSTON

Warner Books

1271 Avenue of the Americas, New York, NY 10020

Printed in the United States of America

First Edition: May 2006
10   9   8   7   6   5   4   3   2   1

Library of Congress Control Number: 2005938970
ISBN: 0-446-57780-4

Book design by Charles Sutherland

Dedication

The true inspiration for this book comes from years of listening to our own inner voices say, "Why couldn't I have done that the first time?" Unfortunately, we aren't the only ones who have said that. Millions of golfers around the world have uttered these exact words or something similar. It seemed only natural to attempt to answer our own question while at the same time serving mankind at large.

Therefore we dedicate this work to all our golfing partners around the world who, like us, over the years, have looked for the secret to eliminating the errant shank, the dead pull, the chili-dip, the blocked shot, and the choked putt, and who, like us, are not ready to quit their day jobs. As August Busch might say: This one's for you.

Acknowledgments

Because this is our first literary effort, the authors would like to acknowledge all the assistance and encouragement they have received from Time Warner Executive Editor Rick Wolff. We also would like to acknowledge our wives, Barbara and Cheryl, for all the hours and days they have had to endure the meticulous and grueling research we had to conduct on golf courses and 19th holes around the country.

—Jim Bronner and Bob Gilhooley

How to Hit the Second

FIRST

Introduction

Golf is a unique sport because a golfer gets only one chance to hit a shot. In tennis a player can miss his first serve and get a second chance; in bowling a bowler gets two bonus balls if he knocks down all the pins on his first attempt and gets a second ball to try to do so if he fails on his first attempt, and if he succeeds the second time he still gets one bonus ball; in football a team has four tries to make a first down; in baseball a batter can accumulate two strikes before he is called out on the third strike; in basketball a shooter can miss, get his own rebound, and shoot again; but in golf once one hits a shot it counts and the golfer is stuck with the result.

Have you ever missed a three-foot putt, pulled the ball back, and sunk the same putt the second time? Have you ever hit a drive into the woods, teed up again for practice, and striped it 280 yards down the middle? Have you hit a sand shot fat, leaving the ball in the bunker, and then hit a shot easily onto the green? If you have played golf for any length of time, you likely will answer yes to all three of those questions. It's just easier the second time. There isn't any golfer who wouldn't pay any-thing—well, maybe not anything, but at least something—to learn to capture the magic each of us possesses in our "second shots."

It is a little known fact, though readily deduced, that one of the reasons (if not the only reason) the pros play so much bet-ter than the rest of us is that they have learned the secrets needed to capture the magic of the second shot. They are se-crets that have been passed along from generation to genera-tion, much the same way Chicago Bears tickets used to be. No matter what you have read or heard, a Scotsman by the name of Angus Mac Tavish was the first to discover the secrets back in 1723. He told a pro, who told another pro, until today we have the PGA Tour. But the secrets are well kept and might be in the process of dying if not for the research of your authors. Those entrusted with the secrets have seen the economic ben-efits of keeping silent, and not one of them wants to reveal the secrets and break their sworn pact.

In fact most golf professionals adhere to another credo that insists they provide instruction to any person seeking it—this despite matters of uncoordination, nonathleticism, or inability to process that golf students may exhibit. In fact they must provide help no matter how pathetic those seeking it may be—kind of like the Hippocratic Oath doctors take but with a whole lot more hypocrisy. So instead of really curing us or sav-ing our proverbial "golf lives," they give us meaningless tips like Yoda: "Fix your grip, align yourself properly, follow through, take a complete back swing, turn," and on and on.

When these earth-shattering tips fail, they try to sell us new clubs or new grips. But they never reveal the holy grail, how to break the Da Vinci Code of golf, that is, the little secrets they know that propel the ball on a trajectory different from our first shots and allow them to chuckle about the game of golf while we remain frustrated and make excuses for our games.

But there is one secret old Angus never told the pros—he kept it only for his Scottish friends and it is a secret guaranteed to lower any golfer's score. The Scots have guarded it closely for years but we have discovered this secret.

There are hundreds of golf jokes. Some are clever. Most are pathetic and not entertaining. But an exhaustive study of those jokes has revealed that the secrets previously known only to the pros and the secret Angus shared only with his Scottish friends is encoded in the best of those jokes. So study the following jokes we have compiled and you will begin to develop the same ability the pros have to chuckle about the game of golf as well as some good material to share with your favorite foursome. But study the jokes with meticulous care and detail and with the eye of a CIA cryptographer and you will learn the secret keys to capturing the magic of the "second shots" judiciously guarded by the pros over the centuries and the guaranteed secret for lowering your scores previously known only to the Scots.

The Puzzle

The secrets of the pros to be revealed in the jokes:

If you want to hit your second shot first
Carefully study the text of this verse.
You can solve this ancient Scottish code
If you assume a detective's mode.

In the jokes are words you must translate
And then arrange in the code template.
When you do you'll unlock the door
To consistently posting a lower score.

Editor's note: If you're still confused, take all the boldfaced words in the text and match them with the blanks in the code template on pages 156 and 157.

The Jokes

Three guys were playing golf **with** a young lady who loved the game but wasn't very **accomplish**ed. Somehow she managed to get on the green on one of the par-3s. It was really **exciting** as she looked over her 25-foot **putt**.

"I've never had a birdie in my life," she explained. "I'll give a blow job to the guy that can help me sink this putt."

The first guy tells her, "Play it about two feet left of the hole because it will break toward the right at the end."

The second golfer disagreed, saying, "Hit it firm and take the break out of it."

The third golfer looked at the 25-footer and said, "It's a gimme!"

A man staggers into an emergency room **with** two black **eyes** and a golf club wrapped tightly around his throat. Naturally the doctor asks him what happened. "Well, it was like this," said the man. "I was having a quiet round **of** golf with my wife, when she sliced her ball into a pasture of grazing cows.

"We went to look for the ball and while I was looking around, I noticed one of **the** cows had something white at its rear end. I walked over and lifted up the tail and sure enough, there was my wife's golf ball . . . stuck right in the middle of the cow's butt. That's when I made my **mistake**."

"What did you do?" asks the doctor.

"Well, I lifted the tail and yelled to my wife, 'Hey, this looks like yours!' "

Jeb was an avid golfer his entire life. As he got into his sixties, he began to have trouble with his eyesight. He didn't want to give the game up, **so** he went to see the family eye doctor. The doctor said there wasn't much he could do, but he knew of a ninety-seven-year-old man, Mark, who still had perfect sight, could see like an eagle. The doctor gave Jeb the old man's name and suggested that Jeb could use him to watch where he hit his golf ball. Jeb, of course, didn't believe the doctor. The old guy was almost a century old, but could see like an eagle? Well, Jeb made arrangements to bring **Mark** golfing. On the first tee, Jeb drove his ball about 200 yards, but of course, he couldn't see where it went.

He asked Mark, "Did you see my **shot**?"

To which Mark replied, "Sure did."

Jeb asked, "Where did it go?"

Mark replied, "I forget!"

This guy has been stranded on a desert island all alone for ten years. One day he sees an unusual speck on the horizon. As the speck gets closer and closer, he sees that it is not a boat, or even a small raft . . . suddenly, emerging from the surf comes this drop-dead-gorgeous blonde wearing a wet suit and scuba gear.

She approaches the stunned guy and asks, "How long has it been since you've had a cigarette?" "Ten years!" he says. She reaches over and unzips a waterproof pocket on her left sleeve and pulls out a pack of fresh cigarettes. He takes one, lights it, and takes a long drag, and says, "Man, oh man! Is that ever good!"

She then asks him, "How long has it been since you've had a sip of bourbon?" Trembling, he replies, "Ten years!" She reaches over, unzips her waterproof pocket on her right sleeve, pulls out a flask, and gives it to him. He opens the flask, takes a long swig, and says, "Wow, that's absolutely fantastic!"

Then she starts slowly unzipping the long zipper that runs down the front of her wet suit, looks at him seductively and asks, "And how long has it been since you've played around?" The guy, with tears in his eyes, replies, "Oh, sweet Lord! Don't tell me you've got golf clubs in there!"

One fine day in Ireland, a guy is out golfing and gets up to the 16th hole. He tees up and cranks one. Unfortunately, it goes into the woods on the side of the fairway. He goes looking for his ball and comes across this little guy with this huge lump on his head and the golf ball lying right beside him. At a loss for **words**, he proceeds to revive the poor little guy. Upon awakening, the little guy says, "Well, you caught me fair and square; I am a leprechaun. I will grant you three wishes."

The man says, "I can't take anything from you, I'm just glad I didn't hurt you too badly," and walks away.

Watching the golfer depart, the leprechaun thinks, *Well, he was a nice enough guy and he did catch me so I have to do something for him. I'll give him the three things that I would want— unlimited money, a great golf game, and a great sex life.*

A year passes and the same golfer is out golfing on the same course at the 16th hole. He gets up and hits one into the same woods, goes looking for his ball and comes across the same leprechaun. He asks the leprechaun how he is and the leprechaun replies: "I'm fine, and might I ask how **your** golf game is?"

The golfer says, "It's great! I shoot under par every time."

The leprechaun says, "I did that for you. And how is **your** money holding out?"

The golfer says, "Well, **now** that you mention it, every time I put my hand in my pocket, I pull out a fifty-pound note."

The leprechaun smiles and says, "I did that for you too. And how is your sex life?"

The golfer looks at him shyly and says, "Well, maybe once or **twice** a week."

The leprechaun is floored and stammers, "Once or twice a week!"

The golfer, a little embarrassed, looks at him and says, "Well, that's not too bad for a Catholic priest in a small parish."

"Well, caddie, how do you like my game?"
"Very good, sir! But personally I prefer golf."

Q. What's the difference between a golf ball and a clitoris?

A. Men will actually look for a golf ball.

Four guys who worked together always golfed as a group at 7:00 A.M. on Sunday. Unfortunately, one of them got transferred out of town and they were talking about trying to fill out the foursome. A woman standing near the tee said, "Hey, I like to golf, can I join the group?" They were hesitant, but said she could come once to **try** it and they could see what they thought. They all agreed and she said, "Good, I'll be there at 6:30 or 6:45." She showed up right at 6:30, and wound up setting a course record with a 7-under-par round. The guys went nuts and everyone in the clubhouse congratulated her. Meanwhile, she was fun and pleasant the entire round. The guys happily invited her back the next week and she said, "Sure, I'll be here at 6:30 or 6:45." Again, she showed up at 6:30 Sunday morning. Only this time, she played left-handed, and matched her 7-under-par score of the previous week. By now the guys were totally amazed, and they asked her to join the group for keeps. They had a beer after their round, and one of the guys asked her, "How do you decide if you're going to golf right-handed or left-handed?" She said, "That's easy. **Before** I leave for the golf course, I pull the covers off my husband, who sleeps in the nude. If his member is pointing to the right, I golf right-handed; if it's pointed to the left, I golf left-handed. "One of the guys asked, "What if it's pointed straight up?"

She said, "Then I'll be here at 6:45."

A man and his wife were both avid golfers. As fate would have it, they died at the same time, and arrived at the Pearly Gates together. St. Pete showed them around, and when they came to the golf course, they were overwhelmed. It was gorgeous! The works . . . fabulous greens, a great clubhouse, and the most magnificent set of clubs in history for each of them. In short, a golfer's dream! As they teed off on the 1st hole, the guy looked at the wife, and said: "If it wasn't for your fucking oat bran, we could have been here years ago."

After a particularly poor game of golf, a popular club member skipped the clubhouse and started to go home. As he was walking to the parking lot to get his car, a policeman stopped him and asked, "Did **you** tee off on the 16th hole about twenty minutes ago?"

"Yes," the golfer responded.

"Did you happen to hook your ball so that it went over the trees and off the course?"

"Yes, I did. How did you know?" he asked.

"Well," said the policeman very seriously. "Your **ball** flew out onto the highway and crashed through a driver's windshield. The car went out of control, crashing into five other cars and a fire truck. The fire truck couldn't make it to the fire, and the building burned down. So, what are you going to do about it?"

The golfer thought it over carefully and responded, "I think I'll close my stance a bit, tighten my grip, and lower my right thumb."

Two friends went out to play golf and were about to tee off, when one fellow noticed that his partner had only one golf **ball**. "Don't you have at least one **other** golf ball?" he asked.

The other guy replied that he only needed one.

"Are you sure?" the friend persisted. "What happens if you lose that ball?"

The other guy replied, "This is a very special golf ball. I won't lose it so I don't need another one."

"Well," the friend asked, "what happens if you **miss** your shot **and** the ball goes in the lake?"

"That's okay," he replied. "This special golf ball floats. I'll be able to retrieve it."

"Well, what happens if you **hit** it into the trees and it gets lost among the bushes and shrubs?"

The other guy replied, "That's okay too. You see, this special golf ball has a homing beacon. I'll be able to get it back—no problem."

Exasperated, the friend asks, "Okay. Let's say our game goes late, the sun goes down, and you hit your ball into a sand trap. What are you going to do then?"

"No problem," says the other guy. "You see, this ball is fluorescent. I'll be able to see it in the dark."

Finally satisfied that he needs only the one golf ball, the friend asks, "Hey, where did you get a golf ball like that anyway?"

The other guy replies, "I found it."

A golfer is ready to tee off, when a golfer in the adjacent fairway hits him square in the face with his golf ball.

"Idiot! Your ball hit me in the eye! I'll sue you for five million dollars!"

The other golfer replied, "I said 'Fore!' "

The first golfer then said, "I'll take **it!**"

A man starts his confession by telling the priest he has sinned by cursing the Lord and taking his name in vain. The priest, who is Irish, asks, "And tell me, my son, what were the grievous and calamitous circumstances that caused you to curse God and use his name in vain?"

The sinner says, "Well, Father, I was playing golf, and I was finishing the best round ever, when on the 18th tee my drive sliced into the rough."

"So surely, after playing such a magnificent round, that is not what caused you to curse God?"

"No, Father, I lucked out and the ball landed on a bare spot. I took my 6-iron and swung and hit the ball well, it landed on the lip of the green and rolled into a sand trap below the green."

"And surely, my son, escaping danger and making a wonderful second **shot** only to have the ball roll back into a trap, that is not what caused you to **take** the Lord's name in vain?"

"No, Father, I took my sand wedge and I dug my feet in and I swung, and sand and ball went into the air and the ball headed straight for the pin and hit the pole and bounced two feet from the hole."

The priest asked, "Is this hole a par-4?"

"Yes, Father," he says.

"And you're hitting **your** 4th shot two feet from the hole?"

"Yes, Father."

"Jesus Christ, man, did you miss the god-damned putt?"

Two retired men were sitting in the bar at their local golf club, after an appalling round in rainy, cold, miserable conditions, with a pint of beer each.

"That was awful today," said the first man, staring at the table through his pint glass.

"Yeah, it was the worst I've ever played," replied the second.

"I wonder," said the first, "do you think they have golf in heaven? I hope so. Just imagine it, the lush rolling hills, **clean**, clear lakes, immaculate greens, perfect conditions for golf. A heavenly course."

The second man looked at him, and thought for a moment. After a minute or so, he spoke. "Well, my sister is a psychic. We could get her to make contact with some people in heaven, find out about the facilities."

"Great," exclaimed the first man.

"Well," continued the second man, "I'll find out, and I'll talk to you next Sunday when we play."

—A week later—

"So, did you speak to your sister?"

"I sure did, and she managed to get in touch with a few folks up in heaven," said the second man. "However, there's good news, and, I'm afraid, there's bad news."

"Well, tell me the good news first," said the first man.

"The good news is that there are awesome golf courses in heaven, just as we envisaged it. Lush hills, crystal-clear lakes, the lot."

"And the bad news?" said the first man, his voice more hesitant.

"The bad news is, you're off the 1st tee at 9:00 A.M. tomorrow morning."

Two young friends learned golf in high school and played a lot together. After high school they got jobs and proceeded to bet with each other. They were pretty equally matched, so first one would win and then the other would win. As a matter of fact, at the end of the year neither was financially ahead of the other. As life went on they made more money at their jobs and increased the size of their bets. Still one would win and then the other would win. As usual, at the end of the year, neither was financially ahead of the other. They became really aged and decided to hang up the clubs but would play one last game for $10,000 as each was independently wealthy. On the 18th tee the match was even. One hit a beautiful drive down the middle and the other sliced into the woods. They looked for the ball for fifteen or twenty minutes and the fellow on the fairway said, "I'm going to hit up!"

"Okay," said the other, "but I'll keep on looking."

The fellow on the fairway hit one of the best shots of his life and the ball rolled to within six inches of the cup. As he approached the green and got his putter from his caddie, the fellow in the woods shouted, "I found it!"

"Hit it, then!" said the fellow on the green.

The guy in the woods hacked at the ball. It bounded off a branch, flew the trap, hit on the apron, rolled onto the green and into the cup. At which the fellow on the green said to his caddie, "What do I do now? I've got his first ball in my pocket!"

"Can you see your way to letting me have a golf ball, Bill?" Stoney asked his old friend.

"But Stoney, you said you were going to stop playing golf," said Bill reluctantly, handing over an old spare.

"By degrees, Bill. By degrees," replied Stoney, pocketing the ball. "My first step has been to stop buying my own balls."

A foursome is waiting at the men's tee while another foursome of ladies is hitting from the ladies' tee.

The ladies are taking their time, and when finally the last one is ready to hit the ball, she hacks it about 10 feet, goes over to it and hacks it another 10 feet. She looks up at the men who are watching and says, apologetically: "I guess all those fucking lessons I took this winter didn't help."

One of the men immediately replies, "No, you see that's your problem. You should have taken golf lessons instead."

A hack golfer spends a day at a plush country club, playing golf and enjoying the luxury of a complimentary caddie. Being a hack golfer, he plays poorly all day. Round about the 18th hole, he spots a lake off to the left of the fairway. He looks at the caddie and says, "I've played so poorly all day, I think I'm going to go drown myself in that lake."

The caddie looks back at him and says, "I don't think you can keep your head down that long."

Stevie Wonder and Tiger Woods are in a bar. Woods turns to Wonder and says, "How is the singing career going?"

Stevie Wonder replies, "Not too bad! How's the golf?"

Woods replies, "Not too bad. I wasn't **swinging** very well, but I think I've got that right now."

Stevie Wonder says, "I always find that when my swing goes wrong, I need to stop playing for a while and not think about it. Then, the next time I play, it seems to be all right."

Tiger Woods says, "You play golf?"

Stevie Wonder says, "Oh yes, I've been playing for years."

And Woods says, "But you're blind. How can you play golf if you're blind?"

Wonder replies, "I get my caddie to stand in the middle of

the fairway and call to me. I listen for the sound of his voice and play the ball toward him. Then, when I get to where the ball lands, the caddie moves to the green or farther down the fairway, and again I play the ball toward his voice."

"But how do you putt?" asks Woods.

"Well," says Stevie, "I get my caddie to lean down in front of the hole and call to me with his head on the ground, and I just play the ball toward his voice."

"Woods asks, "What's your handicap?"

Stevie says, "Well, I'm a scratch golfer."

Woods, incredulous, says to Stevie, "We've got to play a round sometime."

Wonder replies, "Well, people don't take me seriously, so I only play for money, and I never play for less than $10,000 a hole."

Woods thinks about it and says, "Okay, I'm game for that. When would you like to play?"

Stevie says, "**Pick** any night you want!"

He was 26-over-par by the 8th hole, had landed a fleet of golf balls in the water hazard, and had dug himself into a trench fighting his way out of the rough, when his caddie coughed during a 12-inch putt.

The duffer exploded.

"You've got to be the worst caddie in the world!" he screamed.

"I doubt it!" replied the caddie. "That would be too much of a coincidence."

Four married guys go golfing. During the 4th hole, the following conversation takes place:

First Guy: "You have no idea what I had to do to be able to come out golfing this weekend. I had to promise my wife that I will paint every room in the house next weekend."

Second Guy: "That's nothing. I had to promise my wife that I would build her a new deck for the pool."

Third Guy: "Man, you both have it easy. I had to promise my wife that I will remodel the kitchen for her."

They continue to play the hole, when they realize that the

fourth guy has not said a word. So they ask him. "You haven't said anything about what you had to do to be able to play this weekend. What's the deal?"

Fourth Guy: "I just set my alarm for 5:30 A.M. When it went off, I shut off my alarm, gave the wife a nudge and said, 'Golf course or intercourse?' and she said, 'Don't forget your sweater.' "

There once was a lawyer who was so fanatical about his golf game that he used to play every day without fail. One morning he had played the 1st hole and was just about to tee off on the 2nd, when he saw the most gorgeous woman he had ever seen putting on the 1st. The lawyer waited until the woman had reached the 2nd tee and asked if she would like to join him and they could finish the round together. To his surprise the woman agreed and they played the remaining holes. Not only was this woman beautiful, she was also a good golfer. When they completed their round, the lawyer told the woman that not only was he a lawyer, but he was also a Cordon Bleu chef and wine buff. He invited her back to his place for a meal and a few drinks. The woman accepted enthusiastically and off they went. Back at the house the lawyer cooked a magnificent meal. In fact it was more than just cooking, it was a performance to behold. They enjoyed good food, good wine, and good conversation. After the meal, the woman repaid the lawyer with the best oral sex he had ever experienced. The lawyer was so taken by the beauty and skill of this woman that he desired her no end. He then asked if she would like to play golf the following morning, to which she agreed. Once again they enjoyed a great game of golf, a magnificent evening meal, and once more the woman performed sensational oral sex on the lawyer.

This went on for three weeks, when the lawyer finally said to the woman, "Listen, the golf and the company have been fantastic, but there are only so many performances a man can take. When are we going to have sexual intercourse?"

"We can't," said the woman.

"Why not?" came the reply.

"Because I'm a transvestite," replied the woman.

"YOU BITCH!" screamed the lawyer. "I can't believe that you've been playing off the ladies' tees for the last three weeks!"

Rules of Bedroom Golf

1. Each player shall furnish his own equipment for play, normally one club and two balls.
2. Play on a course must be approved by the owner of the hole.
3. Unlike outdoor golf, the object is to get the club in the hole and keep the balls out of the hole.
4. For most effective play, the club should have a firm shaft. Course owners are permitted to check shaft stiffness before play begins.
5. Course owners reserve the right to restrict the length of the club to avoid damage to the hole.
6. The object of the game is to take as many strokes as necessary until the course owner is satisfied that the play is complete. Failure to do so may result in being denied permission to play the course again!
7. It is considered bad form to begin playing the hole immediately upon arrival at the course. The experienced player will normally take time to admire the entire course, with special attention to well-formed bunkers.

8. **Players** are cautioned not to mention other courses they have played on or are currently playing to the owner of the course being played. Upset course owners have been known to damage a player's equipment for this reason.

9. Players are encouraged to have proper rain gear along, just in case.

10. Players should assure themselves that their **match** has been properly scheduled, particularly when a new course is being played on for the first time. Previous players have been known to become irate if they discover someone else playing what they consider to be a private course.

11. Players should not assume a course is in shape for play at all times. Some players may be embarrassed if they find the course to be temporarily under repair. Players are advised to be extremely tactful in this situation. More advanced players will find alternate means of play when this is the case.

12. Players are advised to obtain the course owner's permission before attempting to play the back 9.

13. Slow play is encouraged; however, players should be prepared to proceed at a quicker pace, at least temporarily, at the course owner's request.

14. It is considered outstanding performance, time permitting, to play the same hole several times in one match.

15. The course owner will be the sole judge of who is the best player.

16. Players are advised to think twice before considering

membership at any **given** course. Additional assessments may be levied by the course owner and the rules are subject to change at any time. **For** this reason, many players prefer to continue playing on several different courses.

17. Players are cautioned to play the correct hole, as indicated by the course owner.

18. It is considered bad form to reveal your score to other players, **or** even that you have played the course.

My wife said to me, "George, it is about time that you **learn how** to play golf. You know, golf. That's the game where you chase a ball all over the country when you are too old to chase women."

So, I went to see Jones and asked him if he would teach me how to play. He said, "Sure, you've got balls, haven't you?"

I said, "Yes, but sometimes on cold mornings they're kinda hard to find."

"Bring them to the clubhouse tomorrow," he said, "and we will tee off."

"What's tee off?" I asked.

He said, "It's a golf term and we have to tee off in front of the clubhouse."

"Not the barn somewhere?"

"No, no," he said, "a tee is a little thing about the size of your little finger."

"Yeah, I've got one of those."

"Well," he said. "you stick it in the ground and put your ball on top of it."

I asked, "Do you play golf sitting down? I always thought you stood **up** and walked around."

"You do," he said. "You're standing up when you put your ball on the tee."

Well, folks, I thought that was stretching things a little too far, and I said so.

He said, "You've got a bag, haven't you?"

"Sure," I said.

He said, "Your balls are in it, aren't they?"

"Of course," I told him.

"Well," he said, "can't you open the bag and **remove** one?"

I said I suppose I could, but damned if I was going to.

He asked if I didn't have a zipper on my bag, but I told him, no, I'm the old-fashioned type.

Then he asked me if I knew how to hold my club. Well, after fifty years I should have some sort of an idea, and I told him so.

He said, "You take your club in both hands."

Folks, I knew right then he didn't know what he was talking about.

"Then," he said, "you swing it over your shoulder."

"No, no, that's not me, that's my brother you're **thinking** about."

He asked me, "How do you hold your club?" and before I thought, I said, "in two fingers."

He said that wasn't right and got behind me and put both arms around me and told me to bend over and he would show me how.

He couldn't catch me there, because I didn't put in four years with the Navy for nothing.

He said, "You hit the ball with your club and it will soar and soar."

I said I could well imagine.

Then he said, "And when you're on the green . . ."

"What's the green?" I asked.

"No, then you take your **putter** . . ."

"What's the putter?" I asked.

"That's the smallest club made," he said.

That's what I've got, a putter.

"With it," he said, "you put your ball in the hole."

I corrected: "You mean the putter?"

He said, "The ball. The hole isn't big enough for the ball and the putter."

Well, I've seen holes big enough for a horse and wagon.

"Then," he said, "after you **make** the first hole, you go on to the next seventeen."

He wasn't talking to me. After two holes, I'm shot to hell.

"You mean," he said, "you can't make eighteen holes in one day?"

"Hell no, it takes me eighteen days to make one hole and besides, how do I know when I'm in the eighteenth hole?"

He said, "The flag would go up."

That would be **just** my luck.

This young golfer from the U.S. Ryder Cup team manages to sneak his new girlfriend into his room at the team hotel. Once she's inside, he quickly switches out all the lights and they rapidly disrobe and leap onto his bed in a flurry of athletic achievement. After about twenty minutes of wild sex they both collapse back on the bed in exhaustion. The girl looks admiringly across at the golfer in the dim light. His beautifully developed muscles and tanned skin glisten with little beads of sweat as he lies beside her. She's really pleased to have met this guy. At this point the golfer **slowly** struggles up from the bed. He fumbles the lid off a bottle on the bedside table, pours himself a small shot in a glass, and drinks it down in one gulp. Then he stands bolt-upright, takes a deep breath, and, in a surprisingly energetic motion, dives under the bed, climbing out the other side and beating his chest like a gorilla. Then he vaults back on top of the girl and commences a frantic repeat performance. The girl is very impressed with the **strengths** of this second encounter. Somehow the golfer has completely recovered from his previous exhaustion! After nearly half an hour of wild activity in every possible position, the gasping male golfer again crawls out of bed and swallows another shot of the mysterious liquid. Once more he dives under the bed, emerges on the other side, beats his chest, and commences to make love all over again. The girl is just amazed and delighted as the action continues at the **same** blistering pace as before. In the darkness, she can't properly see what kind of tonic is causing these incredible transformations, but she sure likes the effect!

More than an hour later, after another repeat of the strange drinking ritual on his part, and a whole string of ecstatic multiple orgasms on her part, the girl is now feeling rather faint herself. "Just a minute, big boy," she whispers. "I think I need to try some of your tonic!" She tries to **kneel** and pours a small shot of the liquid. She braces herself for some sort of medicinal effect, but actually it just tastes like Coca-Cola. Then she stands up straight, takes a deep breath, and dives under the bed. It was at this point that she smashed straight into the three other exhausted members of the U.S. Ryder Cup team.

Two old friends met at the golf course.

"How's it going?" asked the first guy.

"Not so good," said the second. "My wife's divorcing me."

"Why, that's terrible," said the first. "What happened?"

"I made a five-and-a-half-footer on the 18th green," he replied.

"So what's wrong with making a putt?" the first guy asked.

"It wasn't a putt—it was a brunette."

One mid-afternoon on a sunny day, a golfer tees up his ball. After a few practice swings, he steps up to his ball and gets ready to drive the 1st hole. Just before he swings, a woman in a wedding gown comes running up from the parking lot.

She's got tears streaming down her face. Just as she reaches the raised tee, she screams out, "You bastard! I can't believe it! **How** could you do that?"

The golfer calmly swings with **rhythm** and **fluidity** and drives the ball straight down the fairway. He looks at the woman as he puts his driver back in his bag, and says, "Hey . . . I said only if it's raining."

Ernie Els is doing an after-dinner talk. Finishing up, he says, "And the best thing about them is that they are only two calories, and they keep your breath fresh for up to two hours."

"Ernie?" said a guy at the back. "We asked you to talk about tactics."

This sign was posted at a local golf club:

1. Back straight, knees bent, feet shoulder-width apart.
2. Form a loose grip.
3. Keep your head down.
4. Avoid a quick backswing.
5. **Stay** out of the water.
6. Try not to hit anyone.
7. If you are taking too long, please let others go ahead of you.
8. Don't **stand** directly in front of others.
9. Quiet, please . . . while others are preparing to go.
10. Don't **take** extra strokes.

Well **done.** Now flush the urinal, go outside, and tee off!

Two men were having an awfully slow round of golf because the two ladies in front of them managed to get into every sand trap, lake, and rough on the course. They didn't bother to wave the men on through, and after two hours of waiting and waiting, one man said, "I think I'll walk up there and ask those gals to let us play through." He walked out on the fairway, got halfway to the ladies, stopped, turned around, and came back, explaining, "I can't do it. One of those women is my wife and the other is my mistress! Maybe you'd better go talk to them."

The second man walked toward the ladies, got halfway there, and, just as his partner had done, stopped, turned around, and walked back. He smiled sheepishly and said, "Small world."

A nameless but famous American golfer once went to Japan to play in a tournament.

After a few days out on the course practicing, he was getting bored and the night before the start of the tournament, he found himself in a bar in Tokyo chatting to a beautiful Japanese girl. They had a few drinks; he took her out to a sushi restaurant and invited her back to his hotel room.

They got it on and had a wild night of sex, trying **all** sorts of positions. While they were doing it doggy-style the Japanese girl was writhing around and shouting out, "Kuroshiro ho-ru! Kuroshiro ho-ru!"

The golfer was ecstatic at her orgasmic screaming, and, satisfied, he fell into a deep sleep.

He woke up in the morning to find the girl gone and got up to ready himself for his big day on the golf course.

He met up with his Japanese caddie, had a few **practice** drives and putts and the usual pre-round preparation.

He was pleased to see **that** there was a big crowd waiting for him at the first tee. They were cheering to see this famous golfer but gradually a hush fell and they waited expectantly.

Nonchalantly, and not without a little arrogance, he put his ball down, took a few practice **swings**, and then cracked what he thought was a pretty good 275-yard drive down the first fairway. The crowd started shouting and he was amazed to **hear** them saying, "Kuroshiro ho-ru! Kuroshiro ho-ru!"

Convinced that this was a Japanese phrase of the highest

compliment, he turned to his caddie and asked, "Ruchi, what does 'Kuroshiro ho-ru!' mean?"

"Well, now, Arnie-san," the caddie replied. "It means 'Wrong hole!'"

A Marine drill sergeant wanted to play a round of golf one day, and headed out to his favorite links. Waiting on the 1st tee, he noticed an Air Force commander, also waiting on the 1st tee and also alone. Both being in the armed forces, they decided to play together.

It wasn't long before they were talking about work. They shared boot camp stories, war memories, and jokes about new recruits. It went this way until about the 3rd hole, when the Marine sergeant was finishing a story about a runaway tank, and said, "And you know that the Marines are the bravest men in the armed forces."

The Air Force commander dropped his putter and said, "Just what do you mean by that?"

"Well," the sergeant went on, "who do you send to take new

territory? Who do you send in when you're outnumbered? Who gets the call for the most covert operations?"

The Air Force commander putted out, and angrily said, "Well, while you're hiding in the bushes, who's a clear target in the sky? Who do you call for support? And who is always sent in during a losing battle? Sir, the men of the Air Force are the bravest men!"

This argument lasted for the rest of the round. Both men swearing their men were the bravest, and each had stories to tell to back up their claims.

After they finished, they headed to the clubhouse for a beer, still debating the matter. Finally, the Marine sergeant stood and said, "I've got to head back to camp. Play again next week?"

To this, the Air Force commander replied, "Well, I must apologize. It seems I was mistaken. Anyone who played like you did today and is willing to come back to the same golf course is a much braver man than myself!"

Three aspiring golfers were taking lessons from a pro. The first guy hit the ball far to the right. "That was due to LOFT," said the pro.

The second man hit his ball far to the left. "That too was due to LOFT," said the pro again.

The third golfer took a swing, and the ball just went a few feet and stopped. "Once again, it's LOFT," the pro claimed.

"Well, what exactly do you mean by LOFT?" asked the third golfer.

"Lack of fucking talent," replied the pro.

For her fiftieth birthday, a husband told his wife he wanted to help her become a golfer but first he said she needed to go to the gym for a week to get in shape. She did. Here is her diary:

Dear Diary . . .

Because my husband (the sweet dear) wanted me to tone my muscles for golf, he purchased me a week of personal training at the local health club. Although I am still in great shape (from playing on my high school softball team), I decided it would **be** a good idea to go ahead and give it a try. I called the club and made my reservation with a personal trainer named Bruce, who described himself as a twenty-six-year-old aerobics instructor, and model for athletic clothing and swimwear. My husband seemed pleased with my sudden enthusiasm to get started. Well, the club encouraged me to keep a diary to chart my progress, so here it goes: *Monday:* Started my day at 6:00 A.M. Tough to get out of bed, but found it was well worth it when I arrived at the health club to find Bruce waiting for me. He is something of a Greek god— with blond hair, dancing eyes, and a dazzling white smile. Woo Hoo! Bruce gave me a tour and showed me the machines. He took my pulse after five minutes on the treadmill. He was alarmed that my pulse was so fast, but I attribute it to standing next to him in his lycra aerobics outfit. I enjoyed watching the skillful way in which he conducted his aerobics class after my workout today. Very inspiring. Bruce was encouraging as I did my sit-ups, although my gut was already aching from holding it in the whole time he was around. This is going to be a FANTASTIC week!

Tuesday: I drank a whole pot of coffee, but I finally made it out the door. Bruce made me lie on my back and push a heavy iron bar into the air—then he put weights on it! My legs were a little wobbly on the treadmill, but I made the full mile. Bruce's rewarding smile made it all **worthwhile**. I feel GREAT! It's a whole new life for me.

Wednesday: The only way I can brush my teeth is by lying on the toothbrush on the counter and moving my mouth back and forth over it. I believe I have a hernia in both pectorals. Driving was okay as long as I didn't try to steer or stop. Bruce was impatient with me, insisting that my screams bothered other club members. His voice is a little too perky for early in the morning and when he scolds, he gets this nasally whine that is VERY annoying. My chest hurt when I got on the treadmill, so Bruce put me on the stair monster. Why the hell would anyone invent a machine to simulate an activity rendered obsolete by elevators? Bruce told me it would help me get in shape and enjoy golf more. He said some other shit too.

Thursday: Bruce was waiting for me with his vampirelike teeth exposed as his thin, cruel lips were pulled back in a full snarl. I couldn't help being a half an hour late, it took me that long to tie my shoes. Bruce took me to work out with dumbbells. When he was **not** looking, I ran and hid in the men's room. He sent Lars to find me, then, as punishment, put me on the rowing machine—which I sank.

Friday: I hate that bastard Bruce more than any human being has ever hated any other human being in the history of the world. Stupid, skinny, anemic little cheerleader. If there was a part of my body I could move without unbearable pain, I would beat him with it. Bruce wanted me to work on my triceps. I don't **have** any triceps! And if you don't **want** dents in the floor, don't hand me the fucking barbells or anything that weighs more than a sandwich. (Which I am sure you learned in the sadist school you attended and graduated summa cum laude from.) The treadmill flung me off and I landed on a health and nutrition teacher. Why couldn't it have been someone softer, like the drama coach or the choir director?

Saturday: Bruce left a message on my answering machine in his grating, shrilly voice wondering why I did not show up today. Just hearing him made me want to smash the machine with my planner. However, I lacked the strength to even use the TV remote and ended up catching eleven straight hours of the fucking Golf Channel.

Sunday: I'm having the church van pick me up for services today so I can go and thank GOD that this week is over. I will also pray that next year my husband (the BASTARD) will choose a gift for me that is fun—like a root canal or a hysterectomy.

The party games were a triumph and now the marbles tournament was in full swing. Then six-year-old Simon missed an easy shot and let fly with a potent expletive.

"Simon," his mother remonstrated in embarrassment from the sidelines, "what do little boys who swear when they are playing marbles turn into?"

"Golfers," Simon replied.

A murder has been committed.

Police are called to an apartment and find a man standing, holding a 5-iron in his hands, and looking at **the** lifeless body of a woman on the ground.

The detective asks, "Sir, is that your wife?"

"Yes."

"Did you hit her with that golf club?"

"Yes. Yes, I did," the man answers. He stifles a sob, drops the club, and puts his hands on his head.

"How many times did you hit her?"

"I don't know. Five . . . six . . . put me down for a five."

A man and woman are standing at the altar, about to be married, when the bride-to-be looks at her prospective groom and sees that he has a set of golf clubs with him.

"What on earth are you doing with those golf clubs in church?" she whispers.

"Well," he says, "this isn't going to take all afternoon, is it?"

It was a sunny Saturday morning on the 1st hole of a busy golf course **and** I was beginning my pre-shot routine, when a piercing voice came over the clubhouse loudspeaker. "Would the gentleman **on** the women's tee back up to the men's tee, please!" I could feel every eye on the course looking at me. I was so deep in my routine, seemingly impervious to the interruption. Again the announcement, "Would the MAN on the women's tee kindly back up to the men's tee."

I simply ignored the guy and continued to **concentrate**, when once more, the man yelled, "Would the man on the women's tee back up to the men's tee, please!" I finally stopped, turned, looked through the clubhouse window directly at the person with the mike, cupped my hands, and shouted back: "Would the BITCH in the clubhouse kindly shut the fuck up and let me play my second shot!"

Snead, Jones, and Hogan are standing before God at the throne of heaven. God looks at them and says, "Before granting you a place at my side, I must first ask you **what** you believe in."

Addressing Snead first, he asks, "What do you believe?"

Snead looks God in the eye and states passionately, "I believe golf to be the food of life. Nothing else brings such unbridled joy to so many people. I have devoted my life to bringing such joy." God looks up and offers Snead the seat to his left.

He then turns to Jones and asks, "And you, Jones, what do you believe?"

Jones stands tall and proud. "I believe courage, honor, and

passion are the fundamentals to life and I've spent my whole playing career providing a living embodiment of **these** traits." God, moved by the passion of the speech, offers Jones the seat to his right.

Finally, he turns to Hogan. "And **you**, Mr. Hogan, what do you believe?"

"I believe . . ." says Hogan ". . . you're sitting in my seat."

Wally found the following ransom note slipped under his front door: "If you ever want to see your wife alive again, bring $50,000 to the 17th green at your country club tomorrow at 10:00 A.M."

But it was after 1:00 P.M. by the time he arrived at the designated meeting spot.

A masked man stepped out from behind the bushes and demanded, "You're over three hours late. What took you so long?"

"Give me a break!" said Wally, pointing to his scorecard. "I'm a 27-handicap."

A fellow is getting ready to tee off on the 1st hole, when a second fellow approaches **and** asks if he can join him. The first says that he usually plays alone but agrees to let the second guy join him.

Both are even after the first couple of holes. The second guy says, "Say, we're about evenly matched, how about we play for five bucks a hole?"

The first fellow says that he usually plays alone and doesn't like to bet but agrees to the terms. Well, the second guy wins the rest of the holes and as they're walking off the 18th hole, and while counting his $90, he confesses that he's the pro at a neighboring course and likes to pick on suckers.

The first fellow reveals that he's the parish priest at the local Catholic church, to which the second fellow gets all flustered and apologetic and offers to give the priest back his money. The priest says, "No, no. You won fair and square and I was foolish to bet with you. You keep your winnings."

The pro says, "Well, is there anything I can do to make it up to you?"

The priest says, "Well, you **could** come to Mass on Sunday and make a donation. Then, if you bring your mother and father by after Mass, I'll marry them for you."

A couple is on their honeymoon, lying in bed, about ready to consummate their marriage, when the new bride says to the husband, "I have a confession to make. I'm not a virgin."

The husband replies, "That's no big thing in this day and age. Everyone has **weaknesses**."

The wife continues. "Yeah, I've **been** with one other guy."

"Oh yeah? Who was the guy?"

"Tiger Woods."

"Tiger Woods the golfer?"

"Yeah."

"Well, he's rich, famous, and handsome. I can see why you went to bed with him."

The husband and wife then make passionate love. When they **get** done, the husband gets up and walks to the telephone.

"What are you doing?" says the wife.

The husband says, "I'm hungry. I was going to call room service and get some food."

"Tiger wouldn't do that."

"Oh yeah? What **would** Tiger do?"

"He'd come back to bed and do it a second time."

The husband puts down the phone and goes back to bed to make love with his wife a second time. When they finish, he gets up and goes over to the phone.

"What are you doing?" she says.

The husband says, "I'm still hungry, so I was going to get room service to get some food."

"Tiger wouldn't do that."

"Oh yeah? What would Tiger do?"

"He'd come back to bed and do it one more time."

The guy slams down the phone and goes back to bed and makes love to his wife one more time. When they finish he's tired and beat. He drags himself over to the phone and starts to dial.

The wife asks, "Are you calling room service?"

"No! I'm calling Tiger Woods to find out what's par for this hole!"

A man entered the bus with both of his front pockets full of golf balls and sat down next to a beautiful blonde. The blonde kept staring at him and his bulging pockets. Finally, uncomfortable after many such glances from her, he said, "Golf balls." Nevertheless the blonde continued to glance and him and finally, not being able to contain her curiosity any longer, asked: "Does it hurt as much as tennis elbow?"

Q. What is the worst golf foursome?

A. O. J. Simpson, Ted Kennedy, Monica Lewinsky, and Bill Clinton.

Q. Why?

A. O. J. slices, Kennedy can't go near the water, Monica hooks, and Bill does not know what hole he is on.

Two men were out playing a game of golf. One of them was teeing off at the 3rd hole, when a beautiful naked lady ran past. Naturally this distracted him somewhat, but the true committed golfer that he was, he resumed his stance. As he was about to hit the shot again, two men in white coats ran past. "What's going on here?" he thought, once again taking his stance. Another distraction as a third man went running by in a white coat, but this man was carrying two buckets of sand.

Eventually, he was ready again, and took his shot. As he was walking down the fairway, he asked his companion what he thought had been going on.

His companion knew and told him: "Well, that lady once a week manages to escape from the mental hospital beside the course, tears off her clothes, and runs across the fairways. The three guys you saw were the nurses. They have a race to see which can catch her first, and the winner gets to carry her back."

"What about the bucket of sand?"

"Well, that guy won last week, the buckets of sand are his handicap."

A man and his teenage son stop at a drugstore on the way to the golf course. As they are walking through the store the teenager spots the condom section. He says, "Dad, what is the three-pack for?" The dad says, "That is for high school kids—two for Friday and one for Saturday." The son then says, "What is the six-pack for?" The dad says, "That is for college kids—two for Friday, two for Saturday, and two for Sunday." Finally, the son says, "What is this twelve-pack for?" The dad answers: "That is for married couples—one for January, one for February, one for March . . ."

A guy went out on the golf course and took a high-speed ball right **in** the crotch. Writhing in agony, he fell to the ground. When he finally got himself to the doctor, he said, "How bad is it, Doc? I'm getting married next week, and my fiancée is still a virgin in every way." The doc said, "I'll have to put your penis in a splint to let it heal and keep it straight. That should **eliminate** the problem by next week." So he took **four** tongue depressors and formed a neat little four-sided bandage, and wired it all together; an impressive work of art. The guy mentioned none of this **to** his girl. They got married and on the honeymoon night in their hotel room, she rips open her blouse to reveal a gorgeous set of breasts. This was the first time he saw them, and she said, "You'll be the first; no one has ever touched them before." He tore off his pants and underwear. Trying to match her virtue he says, "Look at this. It's still in the crate."

The Top 10 Things in Golf That Sound Dirty

10. Look at the size of his putter.
9. Oh, dang, my shaft's all bent.
8. You really whacked the hell out of that sucker.
7. After 18 holes I can barely walk.
6. My hands are so sweaty I can't get a good grip.
5. Lift your head and spread your legs.
4. You have a nice stroke, but your follow-through leaves a lot to be desired.
3. Just turn your back and drop it.
2. Hold up. I've got to wash my balls.

And the number one thing in golf that sounds dirty . . .

1. Damn, I missed the hole again.

A woman playing golf was stung by a bee. Afraid she'd have an allergic reaction, she ran back to the clubhouse to find the pro. Finding him, she said breathlessly, "I've been stung by a bee! What shall I do?" "Where were you stung?" the pro asked. "Between the 1st and 2nd holes!" "Lady, we gotta work on your stance."

Bob, a 24-handicapper, arrived at the 1st tee with his regular partners. He took his driver and nailed it straight down the fairway like he had never done before. His playing partners looked on in amazement but said nothing.

On approaching his ball, Bob took out a short iron and knocked the ball onto the middle of the green and then proceeded to calmly 2-putt for par. Again, nothing was said other than, "Well played, Bob."

This sequence continued for the next five holes, with Bob even par through six.

The 7th was the number one handicap hole—a really long and difficult par-4 of some 440 yards. Again, Bob drilled one down the middle an unprecedented distance of 250 yards. By this stage, his playing partners' curiosity got the better of them and they asked him how he had done that.

Bob replied that he had just changed to new bifocal glasses and when he looked down to **address** the ball he could see a big club and a little club, a big ball and a little ball, so he hit **the** little **ball** with the big club—easy!

With 170 left to the green, Bob selected a 7-iron and floated it right into the heart of the green. Turning to his partners, Bob said, "See, big club, little club, big ball, little ball—I hit the little ball with the big club—easy!"

Bob lined up his putt. It was a real animal—a 35-footer with a double-break over a ridge to the hole tucked away at the back of the green. Calmly, Bob stroked the putt and it sped into the cup without touching the sides. Birdie!

Stunned silence from his partners **until** one asked, "How can **you** do that on your handicap?"

Bob's response was swift: "I told you—these new glasses are great, I saw a big ball and a little ball, looked up along the **line** and saw a big hole and a little hole, so I hit the little ball into the big hole."

On the next hole, Bob disappeared from the group for a few

moments, and on his return one of his partners observed that Bob's slacks were wet. He inquired, "What happened, Bob?" to which Bob replied, "I went into the bush for a quick leak and when I looked down I saw a big one and a little one. I knew the big one wasn't mine, so I put **it** away."

A fellow was playing a round on a quiet day at his local course; just he and his wife as caddie. On the par-4 7th hole he slices the ball and it comes to rest near an old barn, which stands between his ball and the hole.

He takes out his 9-iron to chip back onto the fairway, when his wife says, "Don't do that, dear. **If** I open the barn doors on your side **and** I open the doors near the fairway, **you** can see the fairway and play onto the green."

"Great idea, wifey!" says he, and he replaces the 9-iron with a 4-iron and proceeds to play his shot through the barn. He takes a tremendous swipe and the ball moves at a great pace, but just as it is about to leave the barn, it hits one of the exposed beams, ricochets, and hits his wife on the side of the head, and she is dead before she hits the ground.

Some months pass and he plays no golf, but is eventually

convinced **by** a few guys to come out and make **up** a foursome. On the 7th hole he slices yet again, and lands near the old barn.

He takes out his 9-iron, ready to chip back out onto the fairway, **when** one of his friends says to him, "Why don't I open the barn doors on my side, **you** do the same and you'll **have** a clear shot to the green?"

The fellow began to **stare** at him **somberly** and says: "I can't do that."

"Why not?" says his friend.

"Well," he says in a low and breaking voice, "You know what happened last time I did that, don't you?"

"No, what happened?" his friend replies.

"Well, the last time I played this shot . . . I got a 7."

There was a foursome of ladies about to play a par-3, 165 yards long.

Suddenly, out from the trees beside the fairway a streaker ran across the open expanse of the fairway. In a gasp, one lady remarked, "I think I know that guy. Isn't that Dick Green?"

"No," replied another. "I think it's a reflection of the grass!"

Their regular foursome teed off on time that Saturday morning. On the 2nd hole Joe noticed a funeral procession going by and stopped, held his hat over his heart, and bowed his head. His partners noticed and complimented Joe on his thoughtfulness. "She was a good wife for forty years," replied Joe.

A young golfer was playing in his first PGA Tour event. After his **practice** round he noticed a beautiful young lady by the clubhouse. He went up to her, began talking, and convinced her to come back to his hotel room for the night. All through the night they made wild love together.

In the morning, the woman woke up and arose **from** bed.

The man said, "Please don't go. I love you and I want you to stay with me."

The woman replied, "You don't understand . . . I'm a hooker."

The man said, "**That's** no problem, you probably just have too strong a grip."

The pro is teaching a young woman how to play and they're working on her grip. After she repeatedly duffs shots, the pro says, "You have a death-grip on the **club** and it's killing **your** power. Just hold the club the same way you would hold **your** husband's penis."

The lovely young thing proceeds to hit a drive 200 yards down the middle!

The pro says, "Great shot! Now, take the club out of your mouth . . ."

Morris was a man who knew all there was to know about golf. He knew all the courses, the champions, their scores, as well as the prize money the professionals had won for the past fifty years. He had read every book ever published on the game and knew all there was to know about technique, but, strange to say, he had never played a game.

Having listened to him hold forth for so long, his friends finally ganged up on him and insisted that he play a game. It was arranged for the following weekend. Morris set out with borrowed clubs and faced the 18 holes of his home course.

Five hours later he returned with a score of 53, which included four eagles, nine birdies, and a hole in one. Never had anyone seen such a fine performance from a beginner. However, while the celebrations were going on in the clubhouse, Morris announced that he would never play again.

"What?" cried his distraught friends.

"What?" cried the equally distraught pro. "But you could win all sorts of prizes for the club. You know everything there is to know about the game."

"Not everything," Morris replied. "The books didn't tell me I'd have to walk!"

A man was golfing one day and was struck by lightning. He died and went to heaven. St. Peter told him when he arrived at the gates of heaven that the bolt of lightning was actually meant for his golf partner. But, because God doesn't want it known that he makes **mistakes**, the man would have to go back to earth as someone other than himself.

Well, the man thought about it for a while and announced to St. Peter that he wanted to return to earth as a lesbian.

St. Peter asked the man why a macho guy like him would choose to return as a lesbian. The man answered, "It's simple, really. This way I can still make love to a woman, AND I can hit from the red tees."

A man takes the day off from work and decides to go out golfing.

He is on the 2nd hole, when he notices a frog sitting next to the green. He thinks nothing of it and is about to shoot, when he hears, "Ribbit. 9-iron." The man looks around and doesn't see anyone. "Ribbit. 9-iron."

He looks at the frog and decides to prove the frog wrong, puts his other club away, and grabs a 9-iron. Boom! He hits it 10 inches from the cup. He is shocked. He says to the frog, "Wow that's amazing. You must be a lucky frog, eh?" The frog replies, "Ribbit. Lucky frog."

The man decides to take the frog **with** him to the next hole. "What do you think, frog?" the man asks. "Ribbit. 3-wood." The guy takes out a 3-wood and boom! Hole in one. The man is befuddled and doesn't know what to say. By the end of the day, the man has golfed the best game of his life and asks the frog, "Okay, where to next?" The frog replies, "Ribbit. Las Vegas."

They go to Las Vegas and the guy says, "Okay, frog, now what?" The frog says, "Ribbit. Roulette." Upon approaching the roulette table, the man asks, "What do you think I should bet?" The frog replies, "Ribbit. $3,000, black 6." Now, this is $10,000 and a long shot to win, but after the golf game, the man figures what the heck. Boom! Tons of cash come sliding back across the table.

The man takes his winnings and buys the best room in the hotel. He sits the frog down and says, "Frog, I don't know how to repay you. You've won me all this money and I am forever grateful." The frog replies, "Ribbit. Kiss me." He figures, why not, since after all the frog did for him he deserves it. With a kiss, the frog turns **into** a gorgeous fifteen-year-old girl.

"And that, your honor, is how **the** girl ended up in my room."

A foursome of elderly ladies came back after a round of golf. At the 19th hole in the clubhouse, the pro asked them, "How did your game go?"

The first said that she had a good round with 25 riders. The second said she did okay with 16 riders. The third said not too bad with only 10 riders. The fourth was disappointed and said that she had played badly with only 2 riders.

The pro was confounded by this term "rider," but, not wanting to show his ignorance, he just smiled and wished them better golf luck next time. He then approached Jerry the bartender and asked, "Jerry, can you tell me what does this term 'riders' mean?"

Jerry smiled and said, "That's easy. A 'rider' is when you hit a shot long enough to take a ride on a golf cart."

Man and woman at the breakfast table, she having a cup of coffee, he reading the newspaper. Wife to husband: "Honey, if I die before you, will you remarry?"

Husband, quietly putting the paper down, a little surprised, replies: "Well, we have had a **good** marriage, and marriage is a good institution . . . so, yes, I'd probably remarry."

He goes back to reading the paper, she gets another cup of coffee, and, after a few minutes, asks: "Honey, if I die before you, and you remarry, would you bring her to live in our house?"

He lowers the paper **slowly**, thinks for a second, and says: "Well, we worked hard to pay off the mortgage and it would be silly to move someplace else, so, yes, I think I would bring her to live here."

He returns to his paper, a few minutes pass and she asks: "Honey, if I die before you and you remarry and you bring her to live here in our house, would you let her use my golf clubs?"

"Don't be ridiculous," he says as he slams down the paper. "She's a lefty."

"Okay, take a swing without hitting the ball," the golf pro said as he began a lesson with his new student.

"But that's exactly what I'm trying to correct!" said the student.

While playing a round of golf one day, Bill hit a shot into the middle of a field of buttercups. As he was preparing to hit his next shot (probably uprooting most of the buttercups), a voice out of nowhere said, "Please don't hurt my buttercups." Bill, not sure he heard correctly, prepared to hit his shot anyway.

Again a voice asked him not to hurt the buttercups. Bill placed his ball back on the fairway to make his shot, and instantly Mother Nature appeared. "Thank you for not hurting my buttercups. As a reward I will give you a year's supply of butter!"

Bill was momentarily surprised and then he became angry. "Thanks a lot, lady, but where were you when I was stuck in the pussy willows!"

A guy comes home really late from his day at the course. His tee time was 1:04 and he was supposed to be home at 6:00 for supper with his wife and kids. His wife greets him at the door at 11:30 and says, "Where the hell have you been?"

He quickly replies, "Well, I finished my round with the boys and I played really well and won all the cash. So I decided to buy the guys a few drinks. After a couple each they had to leave. However, the waitress overheard about my great round, so then she buys me a few shots. We made some small talk and then out of the blue she invites me back to her place. Next thing you know we get back to her place, she starts pulling off my clothes, kissing me passionately, and we end up making love to each other for a couple of hours and now here I am!"

His wife looks him square in the eye and says, "You lying bastard, you played another 18, didn't ya!!!!"

"Well, I have never played this badly before!"
"I didn't realize you had played before, sir."

The bank manager of the local bank noticed one of his co-members would come to the bank every Monday morning and deposit $10,000, never more, never less. This went on week after week and it aroused the manager's curiosity. The next Sunday he saw the man near the 1st tee with a few Asian guests and approached him. The manager commented, "I cannot help but notice that every Monday morning you come to my bank and deposit $10,000. You must have a very reliable business. May I ask what it is?"

The man responded, "Oh, I'm just a gambler."

This surprised the manager even more; he had seen the man play and was not at all impressed with his game. Nevertheless he said, "You must be good, or have a special system, I did not think there was that much to win on the course."

The man came back: "Well, I do not really bet on golf, but a lot of people come here who will bet on anything. Let me give you an example: I will bet you $10,000 that by bank opening Monday your testicles will be square."

The manager was dumbfounded. He had never heard anything so crazy and immediately accepted the bet. Rubbing his hands in anticipation he went off for his game, but all day kept putting his hands in his pocket to check out his equipment. Game over, he went home, had a bath, and was happy to see all was normal. The next morning he set off for the bank early, still satisfied all was okay, waited, and ten minutes before opening the gambler came along with an old Asian man. The manager, smiling, let him in and advised, "You owe me $10,000, they are still round."

The man said "Okay, no problem, but I am sure you will not mind if I check."

The manager did not hesitate, so the gambler undid his fly, slid his hand in, and checked his things. Just at that time the older gentleman collapsed on the floor. "My God, what is wrong with your friend?" queried the manager.

"Nothing, really," answered the man. "It's just that I bet him $20,000 I could play with the bank manager's balls before opening on Monday."

A pastor, a doctor, and an engineer were waiting one morning for a particularly slow group of golfers.

Engineer: "What's with these guys? We must have been waiting for fifteen minutes!"

Doctor: "I don't know, but I've never seen such ineptitude!"

Pastor: "Hey, here comes the greenskeeper. He keeps no **secrets.** Let's have a word with him. [dramatic pause] Hi, George. Say, what's with that group ahead of us? They're rather slow, aren't they?"

George: "Oh, yes, that's a group of blind firefighters. They lost their sight saving our clubhouse from a fire last year, so we always let them play for free anytime."

The group was silent for a **moment**.

Pastor: "That's so sad. I think I will say a special prayer for them tonight."

Doctor: "Good idea. And I'm going to contact my ophthalmologist buddy and see if there's anything he can do for them."

Engineer: "Why can't these guys play at night?"

Four married guys go golfing on Sunday. During the 3rd hole the following conversation ensues:

First Guy: "Man, you have no idea what I had to do to be able to come out golfing this weekend. I had to promise my wife that I will paint every room in the house next weekend."

Second Guy: "That's nothing, I had to promise my wife that I will build her a new deck for the pool."

Third Guy: "Man, you both have it easy! I had to promise my wife that I will remodel the kitchen for her."

They continue to play the hole, when they realize that the fourth guy has not said a word. So they ask him. "You haven't said anything about what you had to do to be able to come golfing this weekend. What's the deal?"

Fourth Guy: "I don't want to talk about it. Let's just say that the foundation for the new house is being poured next Tuesday."

A young man who was also an avid golfer found himself with a few hours to spare one afternoon. He figured if he hurried and played very fast, he could get in nine holes before he had to head home. Just as he was about to tee off, an old gentleman shuffled onto the tee and asked if he could accompany the young man, as he was golfing alone. Not being able to say no, he allowed the old gent to join him.

To his surprise the old man played fairly quickly. He didn't hit the ball far, but plodded along consistently and didn't waste **much** time. **Finally,** they reached the 9th fairway and the young man found himself with a tough shot. There was a large pine tree right in front of his ball—and directly between his ball and the green.

After several minutes of debating how to hit the shot the old man finally said, "You know, when I was your age I'd hit the ball right over that tree."

With that challenge placed before him, the youngster swung hard, hit the ball up, right smack into the top of the tree trunk, and it thudded back on the ground not a foot from where it had originally lay.

The old man offered one more comment, "Of course, when I was your age that pine tree was only three feet tall."

Two women were playing golf. On the 3rd hole there was a foursome of men in front of them but about 175 yards down the fairway. The first woman said, "I'll tee off. They're far enough away." She hit the drive of her life, like a shot, straight down the fairway. She screamed, "Fore!" at the top of her lungs. As the men turned, one was hit solidly. He was rolling on the ground in pain with his hands between his legs.

She ran to him, apologizing and saying, "Let me help. I am a physical therapist." He protested but she got him to put his hands at his side. She unzipped his pants and began massaging him.

"How does that feel?" she asked.

He said, "Great, but my thumb still hurts like hell."

Sam and Becky are celebrating their fiftieth wedding anniversary. Sam says to Becky, "Becky, I was wondering—have you ever cheated on me?"

Becky replies, "Oh, Sam, why would you ask such a question now? You don't want to ask that question . . ."

"Yes, Becky, I really want to know. Please . . ."

"Well, all right. Yes, three times . . ."

"Three? Well, when were they?" he asked.

"Well, Sam, **remember** when you were thirty-five years old and you really wanted to start the business on your own and no bank would give you a loan? Remember when one day the bank president himself came over to the house and signed the loan papers, no questions asked?"

"Oh, Becky, you did that for me! I respect you even more than ever, to do such a thing for me. So, when was number two?"

"Well, Sam, remember when you had that last heart attack and you were needing that very tricky operation, and no surgeon would touch you? Then remember how Dr. DeBakey came all the way up here, to do the surgery himself, and then you were in good shape again?"

"I can't believe it, Becky, that you should do such a thing for me, to save my life! I couldn't have a more wonderful wife. To do such a thing, you must really love me, darling. I couldn't be more moved. So, all right then, when was number three?"

"Well, Sam, remember a few years ago, when you really wanted to be president of the golf club and you were seventeen votes **short**?"

A man is playing 18 holes one morning and hits a shot that lands in the middle of the fairway. He goes to his bag and pulls out a 5-iron. Right as he's about to swing, his caddie stops him.

"What are you doing?" the golfer asks. "This is a perfect shot for a 5-iron."

The caddie shakes his head and says, "Trust me. I've worked this course for ten years and you really want to use a 7-iron." The golfer shrugs and concedes, taking the 7-iron from the bag. He lines up and takes his shot. The ball takes an awkward slice, curving through the woods and crashing through a window in the clubhouse. It then ricochets off a wall and strikes his wife in the head, killing her.

The golfer is dismayed. He gives up the sport altogether, abandoning his clubs and shutting himself away in his home. Finally, after a year of soul-searching, he gathers up the courage to go back to the golf course. Several hours later, he finds himself on the same hole, at nearly the exact same spot on the fairway. He reaches for his 5-iron, when up comes the same caddie from the year before.

"Look," the caddie says. "I've been working here for eleven years. Trust me when I say you want to use a 7-iron." The golfer goes ballistic.

"Are you serious, you asshole?" the golfer says. "You gave me the exact same advice a year ago and I didn't even come *close* to hitting the green!"

The Pope met with the College of Cardinals to discuss a proposal from Shimon Peres, the former leader of Israel. "Your Holiness," said one of the cardinals, "Mr. Peres wants to determine whether Jews or Catholics are superior, by challenging you to a golf match." The Pope was greatly disturbed, as he had never held a golf club in his life.

"Not to worry," said the cardinal, "we'll call America and talk to Jack Nicklaus. We'll make him a cardinal, he can play Shimon Peres . . . We can't lose!" Everyone agreed it was a good idea. The call was made and, of course, Jack was honored and agreed to play.

The day after the match, Nicklaus reported to the Vatican to inform the Pope of his success in the match. "I came in second, Your Holiness," said Nicklaus.

"Second!" exclaimed the surprised Pope. "You came in second to Shimon Peres?"

"No," said Nicklaus. "Second to Rabbi Woods."

A man and his friend meet at the clubhouse and decide to play a round of golf together. The man has a little dog with him and on the 1st green, when the man holes out a 20-foot putt, the little dog starts to yip and stands up on its hind legs.

The friend is quite amazed at this clever trick and says, "That dog is really talented! What does he do if you miss a putt?"

"Somersaults," says the man.

"Somersaults?" says the friend. "That's incredible. How many does he do?"

"Hmmm," says the man. "That depends on how hard I kick him in the ass."

Bill and Ralph, both of equal ability, decide to have a round together and "play it as it lays" on all shots. Both hit their tee shots on the par-5 number 1 hole down the middle and about 260. They drive up for the second shot, and Bill hits his shot down the middle for an easy approach. But Ralph slices his over the trees and it ends up in the cart path of the adjoining hole.

"Guess I get a free drop from the cart path," he says.

"Oh no," says Bill. "We agreed. Play it as it lays."

So Ralph drives Bill up to his ball in front of the green, drops him off, and drives over to his ball on the cart path. Bill watches in amusement as sparks shower down from the practice swings of his opponent, then in amazement as a perfectly struck shot lands on the green and rolls to within three feet of the pin. Ralph drives back to the green.

Bill says, "Great shot back there! What club did you use?"

Ralph responds, "Your 6-iron."

A businessman was attending a conference in Africa. He had a free day and wanted to play a round of golf. He asked whether there was any course in the vicinity and was directed to one in the jungle.

After a short journey, he arrived at the course and advised the pro that he wanted to play 18 holes.

"Sure," said the pro. "What's your handicap?"

"Well, it's 16," said the businessman. "But I don't see the relevance, since I shall be playing alone."

"No, it's very important for us to know," said the pro.

The pro then called a caddie.

"Go out with this gentleman," said the pro. "His handicap is 16."

The businessman was very surprised at this constant reference to his handicap. However, he paid it no more attention. The caddie picked up the businessman's bag and a large rifle, which he slung over his shoulder. Again the businessman was surprised but decided to ask no questions.

They arrived on the 1st hole, a par-4.

"Please avoid those trees on the left," said the caddie.

Needless to say, the businessman duck-hooked his ball into the trees. He found his ball and was about to punch it out, when he heard the loud crack of the rifle and a large snake fell dead from a tree above his head. The caddie stood next to him with the rifle smoking in his hand.

"That's the most poisonous snake in all Africa," said the caddie. "You're lucky I was here with you."

After taking a bogey on the hole, they moved to the 2nd, a par-5. "Avoid those bushes on the right," says the caddie.

Of course, the businessman's ball went slicing away into the bushes. As he went to pick up his ball, he heard the loud crack of the caddie's rifle once more and a huge lion fell dead at his feet. "I've saved your life again," said the caddie.

The 3rd hole was a par-3 with a lake in front of the green. The businessman's ball came up just short of the green and rolled back to the edge of the water. He had a shot. However, he had to place one foot into the lake to be able to play. As he was about to chip the ball onto the green, a large crocodile emerged from the water and bit off his right leg. As he fell to the ground, he saw the caddie with the rifle propped at his side looking on unconcernedly.

"Why didn't you shoot it?" said the man as he writhed in pain.

"I'm sorry, sir," said the caddie. "This is the 17th handicap hole. You don't get a shot here."

Ralph goes for a quick round of golf, and at the 1st tee, Bill is about to tee off in front of him. Bill takes a brand-new ball out of his bag, unwraps it, and places it on the tee and slices into the trees.

"Damn!" He reaches into his bag and takes out another brand-new ball, unwraps it, and tees it up. Thwack! He then hooks it miles into the bushes.

"Damn!" He stomps back to his bag for another ball, when Ralph approaches him.

"Er, excuse me, but I notice you're losing a lot of brand-new balls. Why don't you use an old one?"

Bill looks at Ralph. "'Cause I've never had one!"

Dick brings a friend to play golf with two of his buddies to complete a foursome. His buddies ask him if his friend can play golf. Dick says that he is very good.

This guy hits the ball on the 1st hole in the bush, so his buddies look at him and say, "You said your friend was a good golfer." Dick says, yes, he is, watch him play. They see the ball come out of the bush and onto the green. This guy takes 2 putts and makes his par.

Second hole, par-3, this guy hits the ball into the lake. The two buddies look at Dick again and say, "You said this guy was good." Dick replies that this guy is a great player.

So he walks into the lake. Three minutes later they can't see the guy. All of a sudden they see a hand come out of the water. They tell Dick to dive into the lake to go get his friend because he's drowning. Dick replies, "No, that means he wants a 5-iron."

"Hey, George, did you hear the awful news about John?" The two golfers were talking over a drink in the club bar.

"No, what happened to him?"

"Well, he had a great round on Wednesday—under 70, I

heard—anyway, he finished early and drove home, and found his wife in bed with another man! No questions asked . . . he just shot 'em both! Isn't it terrible?"

"Could have been worse," George commented.

"How?"

"If he'd finished early on Tuesday, he would have shot me!"

A group of golfers were putting on the green, when suddenly a ball dropped in their midst. One of the party winked at the others and shoved the ball into the hole with his foot. Seconds later a very fat player puffed onto the green quite out of breath and red of face. He looked around distractedly and then asked: "Seen my ball?"

"Yeah, it went in the hole," the joker answered with straight-**faced** alacrity. The fat one looked at him unbelievingly. Then he walked to the hole, looked in, reached down, and picked up his ball. His astonishment was plain to see. Then he turned, ran down the fairway and as he neared his partner the group on the green heard him shout: "Hey, Sam, I got an 11."

Seems a man of the cloth and two of his congregation had booked a tee time, and as they prepared to tee off, the club pro asked if a lone golfer, Glenn, could join them to make a foursome.

After introductions all around, they proceeded to play a fairly enjoyable round. The only problem was the language used by Glenn whenever he hit an errant shot. This embarrassed the two laymen, but nothing was said during the round.

As the three drove home, the conversation came around to next Sunday's activity at church. At this point the minister suggested they should invite Glenn, since, after all, "He seems to know all the words."

A golfer in his sixties is complaining to his friends about his sex life at home. They give him the name of the foremost sex therapist in the nation, who just happens to be in the same city. He calls and sets up an appointment.

"Doctor," he says, "I have a very unusual problem. I am sixty-seven years old and I am married to a young woman who is just thirty-one. We both love each other and enjoy golfing together but in the bedroom we are having problems. My wife simply cannot reach orgasm. Have you any suggestions?"

"Certainly," replies the doctor. "I have heard this many times before and rest assured, the solution is simple."

The golfer breathes a huge sigh of relief and anxiously awaits the sage advice of the doctor.

"Listen carefully to my instructions and follow them precisely. If you do, I am certain this problem will be solved."

"I'm ready," says the golfer.

"Good. First, when you leave here go directly to the mall and find a nice-looking young man in his twenties and bring him home to your house. Pay him to do this. When you arrive at home, take your wife and the young man directly to your bedroom. Give him your 7-iron and ask him to swing it while you and your wife have sex together. I am certain this will cure her problem."

Not wanting to offend this renowned doctor but obviously not convinced of the merits of his advice, the golfer proceeds to the mall, solicits a young man, and brings him home. Shortly thereafter, the young man is vigorously swinging the 7-iron while the May and December couple make love. However, as time passes, there is no elation coming forth from the young wife.

The golfer springs from the bed and immediately calls the doctor. He is furious.

"Doc," he says. "I paid you $2,000 for your advice and it has yielded nothing. I want my money back."

"Take it easy," says the doctor. "Did you follow my advice precisely?"

"Yes I did."

"All right then. I want you to go back to the bedroom. This time put the young man in the bed with your wife and you swing the 7-iron while they make love."

"Are you crazy? What kind of advice is that?"

"If you want to see this through, I suggest you follow my advice."

Reluctantly, the golfer returns to the bedroom and choreographs the scene. The young man and the wife are making passionate love and the golfer is swinging his 7-iron. Within a few minutes his wife reaches orgasm. In fact, she has multiple orgasms for the next hour.

Finally, exhausted, the two sweaty bodies separate and both lie back on the bed, facing the ceiling.

The old golfer is obviously upset. With a fierce look in his eyes he charges the young man, grabs him by the throat, points his finger at him, and says, "Now, that's the way to swing a 7-iron."

I attended a golf convention in Phoenix over the winter and was interested in the result of one particular study performed on golfers; specifically, I was interested in late afternoon league golfers. This study indicated that the single gentlemen who play in these leagues are skinnier than the married ones.

The reason for this phenomenon was quite simple **when** we finally found the answer. The single golfer goes out and plays his round of golf, has a refreshment at the 19th hole, goes home, and goes to his refrigerator. He finds nothing decent there, so he goes to bed. The married golfer goes out and plays his round of golf, has a refreshment at the 19th hole, goes home, and goes to bed. He finds nothing decent there, so he goes to his refrigerator.

A guy stood over his tee shot for what seemed an eternity; looking up, looking down, measuring the distance, figuring the wind direction and speed. He was driving his partner nuts. Finally his exasperated partner says, "What's taking so long? Hit the blasted ball!"

The guy answers, "My wife is up there watching me from the clubhouse. I want to make this a perfect shot."

"Forget it, man. You don't stand a snowball's chance in hell of hitting her from here!"

A husband and wife were out enjoying a round of golf and about to tee off on the 3rd hole, which was lined by beautiful homes. The wife hit her shot and the ball began to slice. Her shot was headed directly at a very large picture window. Much to their surprise, the ball smashed through the window and shattered it into a million pieces. They felt compelled to see what damage was done and drove off to see what had happened.

When they peeked inside the home, they could find no one there. The husband called out and no one answered. Upon further investigation, they saw a gentleman sitting on the couch with a turban on his head.

The wife said, "Do you live here?"

"No, someone just hit a ball through the window, knocked over the vase you see there, and freed me from that little bottle. I am so grateful," he answered.

The wife said, "Are you a genie?"

"Oh, why, yes, I am. In fact, I am so grateful, I will grant you two wishes, the third I will keep for myself," the genie replied.

The husband and wife agreed on two wishes . . . one was a scratch handicap for the husband, to which the wife readily agreed. The other was for an income of $1 million per year forever.

The genie nodded and said, "Done!"

The genie now said, "For my wish I would like to have my way with **your** wife. I have not been with a woman for many years and, after all, I have made you a scratch golfer and millionaire." The husband and wife agreed and after the genie and wife finished, the genie asked the wife, "How long have you been married?"

She replied, "Three years."

The genie then asked, "How old is your husband?"

To which she responded, "Thirty-one years old."

The genie then asked, "How long has he believed in this genie stuff?"

Bill got a call from the coroner, who wanted to talk about his wife's recent death. Bill told him the whole sad story. "We were on the 3rd hole. Sally, my wife, was standing on the ladies' tee about thirty yards ahead of the men's box when I hit my drive. From the sound when the ball hit her head and the way she dropped like a rock, I knew immediately that she was dead. God only knows where the ball wound up."

The coroner replied, "That explains the injury to her head, but what about the Maxfli embedded in her rectum?"

"Oh," said Bill. "That was my provisional."

Fred, playing as a single at St. Andrews, was teamed with a twosome. After a few holes, the twosome finally asked why he was playing such a beautiful course by himself. He replied that he and his wife had played the course every year—for over twenty years—but this year she had passed away and he kept the tee time in her memory.

The twosome commented that they thought certainly someone would have been willing to take her spot. "So did I," he said, "but they all wanted to go to the funeral."

On the day after his Masters victory, Tiger Woods tried to enter a very exclusive golf club. He was stopped at the gate by a security guard who said, "I'm sorry, sir, but this club doesn't allow black people to enter. However, if you would still like to play, there is an excellent public course about a 3-wood down the road."

Tiger, completely shocked, exclaimed, "But I'm Tiger Woods!"

The guard replied, "I'm terribly sorry, but I didn't recognize you! In that case, the other course is an easy 5-iron down the road."

These two couples play golf together regularly at their club, and on the 6th hole, a par-4, the second shot to the green must carry 80 yards over water. One of the women, Mrs. Smith, for over a year could never carry the water, and would always hit into it, totally psyched out by the presence of the water.

Her friend in the group suggested that she might want to see a hypnotherapist, as rumor was that that could be of help in such a situation. So the woman went to a hypnotherapist for four sessions. In those sessions, the woman was hypnotized and the therapist would "plant suggestions" that when playing the second shot on the 6th hole, she would not see water, but rather a plush green fairway leading all the way up to the green.

About six months later, someone at the club asked whatever happened to Mrs. Smith, that she hadn't seen Mrs. Smith playing golf at the club for almost four months now. She was informed that five months earlier, Mrs. Smith had drowned at the par-4 6th!

One morning, a man approached the 1st tee, only to find another guy approaching from the other side. They began talking and decided to play nine holes together.

After teeing off, they set off down the fairway, continuing their chat.

"What do you do?" the first man asked.

"I'm a salesman. What about you?"

"I'm a hit man for the mob," replied the second man.

The hit man noticed that the first guy started getting a little nervous and continued. "Yeah. I'm the highest-paid guy in the business. I'm the best." He stopped, set down his bag of clubs, and pulled out a fancy, high-powered rifle that was loaded with all types of scopes and sights. He then asked the man where he lived.

Still nervous, the man replied, "In a subdivision just west of here."

The hit man placed the gun against his shoulder, faced west, peered into a scope, and asked, "What color roof ya got?"

"Gray."

Then he asked, "What color siding?"

"Yellow."

"You got a silver Toyota?"

"Yeah," replied the first man, who was now completely amazed by the accuracy of the hit man's equipment. "That's my wife's car."

"That your red pickup next to it?"

Looking baffled, the man asked if he could look through the scope.

Looking through the sights, he said, "Hell. That's my buddy Jeff's truck. What the hell is he doing there if I'm—?"

The hit man looked through the scope once more. "Your wife a blonde?"

"Yeah."

"Your buddy got black hair?"

"Yeah!"

"Well, I don't know how to tell you, but I think you've got a problem. They're going at it like a couple of teenagers in there," said the hit man.

"Problem? *They've* got the problem! I want you to shoot both of them! Right now!"

The hit man paused and said, "Sure. But it'll cost you. Like I said, I'm the best. I get paid $5,000 per shot."

"I don't care! Just do it! I want you to shoot her right in the head, then shoot him right in the groin!"

The hit man agreed, turned, and took firing position. He carefully stared into the sights, taking careful aim. He then said, "You know what, buddy? This is your lucky day. I think I can save you $5,000!"

A man and his gorilla are sitting in the clubhouse, when the club champion comes in. "I'll bet you $500 per hole my gorilla can play better golf than you," says the man.

The champion looks at the man, looks at the gorilla, and says, "You're on." And off they go to the 1st tee.

The 1st hole is a long par-4 over water. The man gives the champion the honors. The champion tees up and hits a beautiful drive straight up the middle, over the water, within chipping distance from the green.

"Nice shot," says the man.

The gorilla tees up, booms the drive onto the green, and into the hole! The champ picks up his ball and they head off to the next hole, a beautiful par-5, along the creek with a slight dogleg left.

The gorilla tees up and booms another drive, drawing it just enough to land it on the green, inches from the pin. The champ, humiliated, concedes the hole and the match. They head back to the clubhouse.

As they settle the bet, the champ remarks how well the gorilla plays. "I've never seen anyone drive it as far. By the way, since he aced the 1st hole and I conceded the match before finishing the 2nd, I never got to see how he putts."

"Oh well," says the man. "He putts exactly like he drives!"

Dame Fortune was seldom kind to Sam. Although Sam had a real zest for life he was constantly beset by bad luck. He loved poker but poker did not love Sam; he played the stock market with great anticipation but always seemed to be the one who bought high and sold low. His life seemed to be full of more downs than ups.

His greatest delight was his golf game. Not that Sam was a great golfer; in fact, he never managed to break 100, but the odd shot that somehow ended up in the general area he had in mind was enough to keep his hopes alive. Finally Sam became ill and passed away. But just before he died, he asked that his remains be cremated and his ashes scattered just off the fairway on the 9th hole of his home course.

Accordingly, a gathering assembled to carry out Sam's wishes. It was a bright sunny day and was going well. Then, as the ashes were being strewn . . . a gust of wind came up and . . . blew Sam out of bounds.

At a golf course, four men approached the 16th tee. The straight fairway ran along a road and a bike path fenced off on the left. The first golfer teed off and hooked the ball in that direction. The ball went over the fence and bounced onto the bike path and onto the road, where it hit the tire of a moving bus and was knocked back onto the fairway. As they all stood in amazement, one man asked him, "How on earth did you do that?"

Without hesitation, he said, "You have to know the bus schedule."

Sam and Harry are playing one day. On the 1st hole, Sam hits a wicked slice into the adjoining fairway. The ball hits another player right between the eyes and he drops to the ground.

Sam and Harry rush over to the prostrate man and find him unconscious with the ball lying on the ground between his legs.

Sam screams, "Oh my God, what should I do?"

Harry replies: "Don't move him. If you leave him there he becomes an immovable obstruction and, according to the rules, you are allowed a drop two club-lengths away."

Fred was a moderately successful golfer, but as he got older he was increasingly hampered by incredible headaches. His golf, personal hygiene, and love life all started to suffer. He managed to push on, but when his game turned really sour he sought medical help. After being referred from one specialist to another, he finally came across a doctor who solved the problem.

"The good news is I can cure your headaches. The bad news

is that it will require castration. You have a very rare condition that causes your testicles to press up against the base of your spine. The pressure creates one hell of a headache. The only way to relieve the pressure and allow your swing to work again is to remove the testicles."

Fred was shocked and depressed. He wondered if he had anything to live for, but then figured at least he could play reasonable golf again. He decided he had no choice but to go under the knife. When he left the hospital, his mind was clear, but he felt like he was missing an important part of himself. As he walked down the street, he realized that he felt like a different person. He could make a new beginning, swing free, and live a new life. He went to the club for a drink and as he walked past the pro shop thought, "That's what I need: a new outfit."

He entered the shop and told the salesman, "I'd like some new golf slacks." The salesman eyed him briefly and said, "Let's see . . . size 44 long." Fred laughed. "That's right, how did you know?" "It's my job." Fred tried on the slacks, they fit perfectly.

As Fred admired himself in the mirror, the salesman asked, "How about a new shirt? I've got some great new Nicklaus stock." Fred thought for a moment and then said, "Sure . . ." The salesman eyed Fred and said, "Let's see . . . 34 sleeve and . . . 16 and a half neck." Fred was surprised. "That's right, how did you know?" "It's my job." Fred tried on the shirt, and it fit perfectly.

As Fred adjusted the collar in the mirror, the salesman asked, "How about new shoes, we just got new stock with soft spikes." Fred was on a roll and agreed. The salesman said, "Let's see . . . 9 and a half . . . wide." Fred was astonished. "That's right, how did you know?" "It's my job." Fred tried on the shoes and they fit perfectly.

Fred walked comfortably around the shop and the salesman asked, "How about a new hat?" Without hesitating, Fred said, "Sure . . ." The salesman eyed Fred's head and said, "Let's see . . . 7 and five-eighths." Fred was really impressed. "That's right, how did you know?" "It's my job." The hat fit perfectly.

Fred was feeling great, when the salesman asked, "How about some new underwear, got some great new imported stock." Fred thought for a second and said, "Sure . . ." The salesman stepped back, eyed Fred's waist and said, "Let's see . . . size 36." Fred laughed. "No, I've worn size 34 since I was eighteen years old."

The salesman shook his head. "You can't wear a size 34—every time you swing it would press your testicles up against the base of your spine and give you one hell of a headache."

A man is playing golf with his wife, when she hits a shot that lands on the green, about 30 feet from the cup. The wife steps up, drills it, hooks it, and bounces it off a rock, clips a tree, sideswipes the second rock, and finally sinks it. The husband looks at this and says, "Okay, now you know how to play, let's go home."

An alien spaceship hovered over a golf course. Two aliens were watching a solitary golfer practicing. This was a new golfer and they watched in amazement.

The golfer duffed his tee shot, shanked his second into the rough, took 3 to get out of the rough into the fairway, sliced the next shot into the bushes, and took a putter to get it out the fairway again.

Meanwhile, one alien told the other that he must be playing rt of game and they continued to observe the golfer.

lfer then hit a shot into a bunker by the green. He shots to get out of the bunker and finally onto the ted several times until he finally got into the hole. At this stage, the other alien told his partner, "Wow, now he is in serious **trouble**."

A couple of old guys were golfing, when one said he was going to Dr. Taylor for a new set of dentures in the morning. His friend remarked that he had gone to the same dentist a few years before.

"Is that so?" the first said. "Did he do a good job?"

"Well, I was on the course yesterday when the fellow on the 9th hole hooked a shot," he said. "The ball must have been going 200 miles an hour when it hit me in the groin. That was the first time in two years my teeth didn't hurt."

"You think so much of your old golf game that you don't even remember when we were married," said the pouting wife.

"Of course I do, my dear. It was the day I sank that 30-foot putt!"

An old tramp had wandered leisurely up to the green of the 18th, where he sat himself down among his many coats. He dug among the variety of old bags he was carrying and brought forth with great pomp a handful of dried twigs and two iron rods, which he arranged to form into a holder. From this he hung a pot of water suspended over the twigs.

Members gathering at the clubhouse windows watched as he got his campfire going. The tranquillity of the scene was shattered when a man dashed from the clubhouse and, leaving no room for doubt, ordered the tramp off the course.

"Well, just who do you think you are?" asked the tramp.

"I'm the club secretary," shouted the man.

"Well, listen, sonny," the tramp retorted. "Let me give you some advice. That's hardly the way to get new members."

He'd been playing for twenty years and he'd never managed it—the ultimate goal, a hole in one. As he was chipping away in a sand trap one day and moving nothing but sand, he voiced the thought: "I'd give anything," he said, "anything to get a hole in one."

"Anything?" came a voice from behind and he turned to see a grinning, red-clad figure with neatly polished horns and sharpened tail.

"What did you have in mind?" the golfer inquired.

"Well, would you give up half your sex life?"

"Yes, yes I would."

"It's a deal, then," and the figure faded discreetly from sight.

On the very next hole he did it. The ball just soared from his club in a perfect arc right into the hole. And for good measure, every other hole he played that round he holed in one. As he was putting his clubs away the figure in red appeared once more.

"Now for our bargain," he said. "You remember, you must give up half your sex life."

The golfer frowned. "That gives me a bit of a problem," he said.

"You're not backing out of this," cried the figure with a swish of his tail. "We'd struck a bargain and you agreed to it."

"Yes, of course. But I do have a problem. Which half of my sex life do you want—the thinking or the dreaming?"

When a maharajah was taken suddenly ill during a holiday in the U.S. he was attended by a young intern filling in for the Johns Hopkins surgeon. The maharajah's appendix was deftly removed and the patient was beaming.

"You saved my life," he said to the young man. "Whatever you want shall be yours."

"It was quite simple, really," protested the young surgeon.

"But I am a rich man, I insist," said the princely patient.

"Well, I'd love a new set of matched golf clubs," the young doctor admitted.

"Consider it done," came the stately reply. The surgeon forgot all about this grand promise until some weeks later when he received this telegram:

HAVE YOUR CLUBS BUT SADLY ALL NOT MATCHED STOP FOUR DO NOT HAVE SWIMMING POOLS STOP

Jesus and Tiger Woods are playing golf. It's Tiger's turn to tee off, and he does so on a long par-5. It's a great drive straight up the fairway, and he's about a 7-iron off the green. "Not bad," Jesus says. Jesus then steps up to tee off, and He too hits a great shot, but it's not anywhere near as close as Woods's first shot.

Just as the ball comes to a stop, a gopher pops out of its hole, grabs Jesus' ball in its mouth, and starts to run up the fairway. Before it can get even 20 yards, an eagle swoops down out of the heavens and grabs the gopher in its mouth and flies off toward the green. Just as the ball, eagle, and gopher get above the hole, a lightning bolt strikes out of a cloudless sky and vaporizes both the eagle and the gopher. The ball drops straight down into the hole for a hole in one.

Jesus looks up and says, "Dad! Please! I'd rather do it myself!"

It seems there was this priest who just loved to play golf, but he had been very busy for many months and had not been able to get away to go golfing. Well, one Sunday morning he woke up and felt he just HAD to go golfing. The weather was just beautiful.

He called up the bishop and claimed he had a really bad case of laryngitis and couldn't preach, so the bishop told him to rest for several days. The priest then got out his clubs and headed off for the golf course.

He set up at the 1st hole, making sure no one was there to see him playing hooky, and blasted the ball with his wood. It was a beautiful shot! It went straight and true. It bounced, and bounced (right up onto the green) and rolled its way closer . . . and closer . . . a hole in one! The priest jumped up and down in his excitement, praising the Lord and shouting hallelujahs!

He strutted off to the green, collected his ball, and teed off at the 2nd hole, repeating his performance on the 1st hole, much to his astounded delight.

All this time St. Peter and God had been watching him from the gates of heaven. St. Peter had finally seen enough to pique his curiosity. "Lord," he said, "this priest seems to be a real troublemaker. He ignored his congregation and even lied to go golfing. Now you reward him with a hole in one! Why?"

God smiled, looked over at St. Peter, and said, "I'm punishing him." St. Peter looked very confused and asked God for an explanation. God replied, "Well, after he finishes his game by himself, who can he tell his story to?"

A young man is playing golf with a priest. At a short hole the priest asks, "What are you going to use on this hole, son?"

The young man says, "An 8-iron, Father. How about you?"

The priest says, "I'm going to hit a soft 7 and pray."

The young man hits his 8-iron and puts the ball on the green. The priest tops his 7-iron and dribbles the ball out a few yards.

The young man says, "I don't know about you, Father, but in my church when we pray, we keep our head down."

After church one Sunday, one of the congregants walked up to the priest and said, "Father, is it a sin to play golf on Sunday?"

"My son," said the priest, putting his hand on the man's shoulder. "I've seen you play golf. It's a sin any day."

A rabbi and a priest go golfing with the club pro and his friend. Before the friend gets up to hit the ball, he crosses himself. With that the rabbi leans over to the priest to ask, "What does that mean?"

To which the priest replied, "Not a damn thing if he can't play!"

Three very religious rabbis in black with long beards are playing golf. A guy named Mulhaney wants to play golf and this was the only threesome in which he could play. So he joins the rabbis and plays 18 holes. At the end of the game his score is 104. The rabbis shoot 69, 70, and 71.

He says to them, "How come you all play such good golf?"

The lead rabbi says, "When you live a religious life, join and attend temple, you are rewarded."

Mulhaney loves golf and figures, what do I have to lose? So he finds a temple close to his home, attends twice a week, converts, joins, and lives a holy life.

About a year later he again plays golf with the three rabbis. He shoots a 104 and they shoot a 69, 70, 71.

He says to them, "Okay, I joined a temple, live a religious life, and I'm still shooting lousy."

The lead rabbi says to him, "What temple did you join?"

He said, "Beth Shalom."

The rabbi retorts, "Schmo! That one's for tennis!"

One night a thief breaks into the Valhalla Golf Club's pro shop in the middle of the night. Fumbling through the titanium drivers, he hears a voice say, "Jesus is watching **you**, Jesus is watching you."

He proceeds to fill his bags with the clubs and other expensive merchandise. While making his way to the sweatshirts, hats, etcetera, he hears . . .

"Jesus is watching you."

Baffled, he looks around with his flashlight and sees a parrot.

He looks at the beautiful creature and says, "What kind of jerk would have a bird like you in a pro shop like this?"

The bird cocked his head slightly and replied, "The same one that named the pit bull Jesus!"

It takes real commitment to play on the Royal Nairobi course. It is bounded on three sides by a wildlife reserve, the wildlife of which do not necessarily feel hesitant about grazing on greens or golfers, according to palate preferences.

The young Mormon missionary had great faith even as he sliced his tee shot into a pretty rugged area off the course. He knew he'd find his ball and he did—right between the forelegs of a huge and hungry lion.

As he fell quivering to his knees before the great beast the young man began to pray and to his astonishment the lion knelt also.

"Glory be to God," exclaimed the young evangelist, "a practicing Christian lion."

"Rowrrl," roared the lion. "Quiet while I'm saying grace!"

A country club didn't allow women on the golf course. Eventually, there was enough pressure that they decided to allow women on the course during the week.

The ladies were satisfied with this arrangement, formed a women's club, and became active. After about six months, the club board received a letter from the women's club complaining about the men urinating on the golf course. Naturally, they just ignored the matter. After another six months, they received another letter reminding them of the previous letter and demanding action. After due deliberation they sent the women a letter advising them that they had been granted equal privileges!

"This is the worst golf course I've ever played on!"
"This isn't the golf course, sir! We left that an hour ago!"

"Caddie, do you think my game is improving?"

"Oh yes, sir! You miss the ball much closer than you used to."

"Please stop checking your watch all the time, caddie. It's distracting!"

"This isn't a watch, sir, it's a compass!"

After coming from a long round of golf, his wife kissed him and kissed their son, who came in a few moments later.

"Where's he been?" the husband asked.

"He's been caddieing for you all afternoon," the wife replied.

"No wonder he looks so familiar!"

A retiree was given a set of golf clubs by his co-workers. Thinking he'd try the game, he asked the local pro for lessons, explaining that he knew nothing whatever of the game.

The pro showed him the stance and swing, then said, "Just hit the ball toward the flag on the 1st green."

The novice teed up and smacked the ball straight down the fairway and onto the green, where it stopped inches from the hole.

"Now what?" the fellow asked the speechless pro.

"Uh . . . you're supposed to hit the ball into the cup," the pro finally said, after he was able to speak again.

"Oh great! So NOW you tell me," said the beginner in a disgusted tone.

A woman is cleaning out her attic and comes across a small box. She opens it and finds three golf balls and $250. When her husband comes home she questions him and he finally admits that every time he was unfaithful to her, he put a golf ball in the box. She immediately goes ballistic and starts yelling at him, but as she is doing so she thinks, "Thirty years of marriage and only three golf balls." She calms down and says, "What you have done is terrible, but I'll forgive you. However, I still don't know what the $250 is all about."

Her husband looks up at her timidly and says, "Well, darling, every time I collected a dozen balls I would sell them."

Two dim-witted golfers are teeing off on a foggy par-3. They can see the flag, but not the green. The first golfer hits his ball into the fog and the second golfer does the same. They proceed to the green to find their balls.

One ball is about six feet from the cup, while the other has found its way into the cup for a hole in one. Both are playing the same type of ball—Top-Flite 2—and they can't determine which ball is which.

They decide to ask the golf pro to decide their fate. After congratulating both golfers on their fine shots, the golf pro asks, "Which one of you used the orange one?"

Golfing Laws

1. No matter how bad your last shot was, the worst is yet to come. This law does not expire on the 18th hole, since it has the supernatural tendency to extend over the course of a tournament, a summer, and, eventually, a lifetime.

2. Your best round of golf will be followed almost immediately by your worst round ever. The probability of the latter increases with the number of people you tell about the former.

3. Brand-new golf balls are water-magnetic. Though this cannot be proven in the lab, it is a known fact that the

more expensive the golf ball, the greater its attraction to water.

4. Golf balls never bounce off trees back into play. If one does, the tree is breaking a law of the universe and should be cut down.

5. No matter what causes a golfer to muff a shot, all his playing partners must solemnly chant, "You looked up," or invoke the wrath of the universe.

6. The higher a golfer's handicap, the more qualified he deems himself as an instructor.

7. Every par-3 hole in the world has a secret desire to humiliate golfers. The shorter the hole, the greater its desire.

8. Topping a 3-iron is the most painful torture known to man.

9. Palm trees eat golf balls.

10. Sand is alive. If it isn't, how do you explain the way it works against you?

11. Golf carts always run out of juice at the farthest point from the clubhouse.

12. A golfer hitting into your group will always be bigger than anyone in your group. Likewise, a group you accidentally hit into will consist of a football player, a professional wrestler, a convicted murderer, and a tax agent—or some similar combination.

13. All 3-woods are demon-possessed.

14. Golf balls from the same sleeve tend to follow one an-

other, particularly out of bounds or into the water (see Law 3).

15. A severe slice is a thing of awesome power and beauty.

16. "Nice lag" can usually **be** translated to "lousy putt." Similarly, "tough break" can usually be translated to "way to miss an easy one, sucker."

17. The person you would most hate to lose to will always be the one who beats you.

18. The last three holes of a round will automatically adjust your score to what it really should be.

19. Golf should be given up at least twice per month.

20. All vows taken on a golf course shall be valid only until the sunset of the same day.

21. If you really want to get better at golf, go back and take it up at a much earlier age.

22. The game of golf is 90 percent mental and 10 percent mental.

23. Since bad shots come in groups of three, a fourth bad shot is actually the beginning of the next group of three.

24. When you look up, causing an awful shot, you will always look down again at exactly the moment when you ought to start watching the ball if you ever want to see it again.

25. Any change works for a maximum of three holes—or at a minimum of not at all.

26. No matter how bad you are playing, it is always possible to play worse.

27. Never try to keep more than 300 separate thoughts in your mind during your swing.

28. When your shot has to carry over a water hazard, you can either hit one more club or two more balls.

29. If you're afraid a full shot might reach the green while the foursome ahead of you is still putting out, you have two options: You can immediately shank a layup, or you can wait until the green is clear and top a ball halfway there.

30. The less skilled the player, the more likely he is to share his ideas about the golf swing.

31. The inevitable result of any golf lesson is the instant elimination of the one critical unconscious motion that allowed you to compensate for all your many other errors.

32. If it ain't broke, try changing your grip.

33. Golfers who claim they don't cheat also lie.

34. Everyone replaces his divot after a perfect approach shot.

35. A golf match is a test of your skill against your opponent's luck.

36. It's surprisingly easy to hole a 50-foot putt when you lie 8.

37. Counting on your opponent to inform you when he breaks a rule is like expecting him to make fun of his own haircut.

38. Nonchalant putts count the same as chalant putts.

39. It's not a gimme if you're still away.

40. The shortest distance between any two points on a golf

course is a straight line that passes directly through the center of a very large tree.

41. There are two kinds of bounces: unfair bounces, and bounces just the way you meant to play it.

42. You can hit a two-acre fairway 10 percent of the time, and a two-inch branch 90 percent of the time.

43. Every time a golfer makes a birdie, he must subsequently make two triple-bogeys to restore the fundamental equilibrium of the universe.

44. If you want to hit a 7-iron as far as Tiger Woods does, simply try to lay up just short of a water hazard.

45. To calculate the speed of a player's downswing, multiply the speed of his backswing by his handicap. Example: backswing 20 mph, handicap 30, downswing 600 mph.

46. There are two things you can learn by stopping your backswing at the top and checking the position of your hands: how many hands you have, and which one is wearing the glove.

47. Hazards attract; fairways repel.

48. You can put "draw" on the ball, you can put "fade" on the ball, but no golfer can put "straight" on the ball.

49. A ball you can see in the rough from 50 yards away is not yours.

50. If there is a ball in the fringe and a ball in the bunker, your ball is in the bunker.

51. If both balls are in the bunker, yours is in the footprint.

52. Don't buy a putter until you've had a chance to throw it.

A deaf and mute golfer steps up to tee off on the 1st hole of a course, when a large burly guy yells, "Hey, you! Nobody tees off ahead of Big Ralph." Being deaf, the fellow continues to prepare for his shot, so Ralph runs up, thinking the golfer is being obstinate, and knocks the poor guy to the ground, kicks his ball away, and prepares for his own shot. After Ralph has hit his shot and has proceeded down the fairway after it, the golfer gets up, brushes himself off, waits a moment, and again prepares his shot.

The golfer then hits a beautiful shot straight up the middle of the fairway, striking big Ralph in the back of the head, and knocking him unconscious. He then walks down the fairway, rolls big Ralph over, and holds up four fingers in front of Ralph's face.

A man got a phone call from his wife at work one day and she asked him to stop at the store and pick up some groceries. Reminding her that this was his golf league night, he said he would be happy to go to the store after playing his round of golf.

After playing golf, he stopped at the store and picked up two bags of groceries. He then proceeded to walk out of the grocery store to his Rolls-Royce. Upon reaching his Rolls-Royce he found it difficult to reach into his pocket to pull his keys out to open his trunk, because his arms were full with two bags of groceries.

He saw a beautiful blond woman walking nearby and he asked her, "Could you please do me a favor?"

"Sure," she replied.

He went on to say, "I can't reach into my pocket and get my car keys out to open my trunk and put my groceries away. Do you think you could reach into my pocket and pull my car keys out?"

"No problem," she replied.

When she pulled the keys out, two golf tees also were pulled out as well and fell to the ground. She bent over and picked them up. Looking at the golf tees in the palm of her hand, somewhat quizzically she asked the man, "Gee, what are these for?"

He replied, "Oh, those are to keep my balls in the air while I'm driving."

To which she commented, "Boy, those Rolls-Royce people think of everything."

A golfer, now into his golden years, had a lifelong ambition to play one hole at Pebble Beach, California, the way the pros do it. The pros drive the ball out over the water onto the green that is on a spit of land that juts out off the coast.

It was something he had tried hundreds of times without success. His ball always fell short into the ocean. Because of this he **never** used a new ball on this particular hole. He always picked out one that had a cut or a nick.

Recently he went to Pebble Beach to try again. When he came to the fateful hole, he teed up an old, cut ball and said a silent prayer. Before he hit it, however, a powerful voice from above said, "**WAIT ... REPLACE** THAT OLD BALL WITH A BRAND-NEW BALL."

He complied excitedly, convinced **the** Lord was telling him that he was finally going to achieve his lifelong ambition.

As he stepped up to the tee once more, the voice came down again, "WAIT ... STEP BACK ... TAKE A PRACTICE SWING." So he stepped back and took a practice swing. The voice boomed out again, "LET ME SEE ANOTHER PRACTICE SWING." He swung again. Silence followed.

Then the voice spoke out again. "PUT BACK THE OLD
BALL."

A blonde is standing by the 1st tee waiting for her golf lesson from the resident professional. A foursome of men is in the process of teeing off.

The first golfer addresses the ball and swings, hitting it 230 yards straight down the middle of the fairway. "That was a good shot," says the blonde. "Not bad, considering my impediment," says the golfer. "What do you mean?" says the blonde. "I have a glass eye," says the golfer. "I don't believe you, show me," says the blonde. He pops his eye out and shows her.

The next golfer addresses the ball and swings, hitting it 240 yards straight down the middle of the fairway. "That was a good shot," says the blonde. "Not bad, considering my impediment," says the golfer. "What's wrong with you?" says the blonde. "I have a prosthetic arm," says the golfer. "I don't believe you, show me," says the blonde, so he screws his arm off and shows her.

The next golfer addresses the ball and swings, hitting it 250 yards straight down the middle of the fairway. "That was a good shot," says the blonde. "Not bad, considering my impediment," says the golfer. "What's wrong with you?" says the blonde. "I have a prosthetic leg," says the golfer. "I don't believe you, show me," says the blonde, so he screws his leg off and shows her.

The fourth golfer addresses the ball and swings, hitting it 280 yards straight down the middle of the fairway. "That was a wonderful shot," says the blonde. "Not bad, considering my impediment," says the golfer. "What's wrong with you?" says the blonde. "I have an artificial heart," says the golfer. "I don't believe you, show me," says the blonde.

"I can't show you out here in the open," says the golfer. "Come around here behind the pro shop."

As they have not returned within five minutes, his golfing mates decide to go and see what is holding them up.

As they turn the corner behind the pro shop, sure enough, there he is, screwing his heart out.

A new executive is told by his boss that he is expected to play in the corporate golf tournament next week. Not knowing how to play, he decides he better take a lesson. The club pro advises that they start with the putter and then progress to the short irons before tackling the long irons and woods. The man explains that he has to start with the driver, as he is expected to play in the corporate tournament. The pro relents and tries to teach him as best he can. On the day of the tournament the new exec steps to the 1st tee, a 165-yard par-3 hole. One of his partners suggests on this hole perhaps a 4-iron might be a better choice. The exec explains that he has had only one golf lesson and the driver is the only club he has hit. The exec takes a mighty swing and proceeds to slice the ball right into the woods. After a few minutes the exec finds the ball and once again pulls his driver out of the bag. His partner suggests that he would be better off hitting a short chip back onto the fairway. Again the new exec explains that he only knows how to hit the driver. He proceeds to take a mighty swing, hitting the tree directly in front of him. The ball careens off the tree, striking the exec in the middle of the forehead, knocking him dead.

St. Peter is surprised to see the executive so soon, and asks, "How did you get here?"

"In 2!" he replies.

On completing his third round at the British Open at Lytham St. Anne's in 1969, Gary Player was approached by a spectator who told him that he was amazed at how Player could make his 3-iron shots stop dead on the green, and asked him how he did it. Player responded by asking the spectator how far he usually hit his 3-iron shots. The spectator replied, "Oh, about 120 to 130 yards."

Player replied, "What do you want them to stop for?"

One golfer asked his friend, "Why are you so late in arriving for your tee time?" His friend replied, "It's Sunday. I had to toss a coin between going to church or playing golf." "Yes," continued the friend, "but that still doesn't tell me why you are so late." "Well," said the fellow, "it took over twenty-five tosses to get it right!"

One guy told his friend, "I've invented a new game that is quite a bit like golf."

"That game is not new," said his buddy. "I've been playing it for years!"

An octogenarian who was an avid golfer moved to a new town and joined the local country club. He went to the club for the first time to play but was told there wasn't anybody he could play with because they were already out on the course.

He repeated several times that he really wanted to play. Finally the assistant pro said he would play with him and would give him a 12-stroke handicap. The eighty-year-old said, "I really don't need a handicap, as I have been playing quite well. The only real problem I have is getting out of sand traps." And he did play well.

Coming onto the 18th, the old man had a long drive, but it landed in one of the sand traps around the hole. Shooting from the sand trap, he hit a very high ball, which landed on the green and rolled into the hole!

The pro walked over to the sand trap where his opponent was still standing. He said, "Nice shot, but I thought you said you have a problem getting out of sand traps?"

Replied the octogenarian, "I do! Please give me a hand."

- Golf is a game in which the slowest people in the world are those in front of you, and the fastest are those behind.

- There's no game like golf: You go out with three friends, play 18 holes, and return with three enemies.
- Golf was once a rich man's sport, but now it has millions of poor players.
- An amateur golfer is one who addresses the ball twice: once before swinging, and once again after swinging.

A father spoke to his son: "It's time we had a little talk, my son. Soon, you will have urges and feelings you've never had before. The **tension** will build, your heart will pound, and your hands will sweat. You'll be preoccupied and won't be able to think **of** anything else." He added, "But **don't** worry, it's perfectly normal . . . it's called golf."

The golfer hit his drive into the adjacent water hazard on the 1st hole. He walked over to look for his ball and saw it about six feet out from the shore in shallow water. He took his ball retriever from his bag, extended it, and reached out into the water and got his ball. As he was drying it off, he heard a voice speak to him.

"Hey, mister," the voice said.

He looked around and saw no one. He started back to drop his ball along the ball's line of flight as it went into the hazard.

"Hey, mister," the voice said again.

He looked down amongst the weeds and grass growing by the water and saw a frog. This time he was looking at the frog when it said, "Hey, mister."

"Yeah? What do you want, frog?" he asked.

"Mister, I'm really a beautiful princess but a wicked witch has put a spell on me and turned me into an ugly frog. If you will pick me up and kiss me, I'll turn back into a beautiful princess. Then you can take me home and we'll make wild passionate love for hours," the frog said.

The man reached down, picked the frog up, and put it in his windbreaker pocket. He walked a few yards back down the fairway and dropped his ball preparing for his third shot.

"Hey, mister," the frog called, "aren't you going to kiss me?"

The man took a couple of practice swings with his 3-wood and then hit the ball onto the par-4 green. Walking on toward the green, he said, "No, I'm not going to kiss you. At my age I'd rather have a talking frog."

What is the similarity between 4-putting and masturbation?

You are slightly ashamed of what you have done and worst of all you know it will happen again!

Jim and Bob are golfing one fine day, when Jim, an avid golfer, slices his ball deep into a wooded ravine. Jim takes his 8-iron and proceeds down the embankment into the ravine, in search of his lost ball. The brush is quite thick, but Jim searches diligently for his errant ball. Suddenly Jim spots something shiny. As he nears the location of the shiny object, Jim realizes that it is an 8-iron in the hands of a skeleton lying near an old golf ball.

Jim excitedly calls for his partner Bob. "Hey, Bob, come here, I got trouble down here."

Bob comes running over to the edge of the ravine and calls out to Jim, "What's the matter, Jim?"

Jim shouts back in a nervous voice, "Bring me my 7-iron. You can't get out of here with an 8."

Joe had a particularly bad day on the course—nothing went right and he became angrier with each passing hole. By the par-3 17th, he was fit to be tied and when he missed a 2-foot putt for a double-bogey, he really exploded.

Letting loose a stream of curses the like of which had never been heard before or since, Joe proceeded to toss his clubs into the lake and set his golf cart on fire. Declaring that he would never play this game again, Joe stomped off to the clubhouse, into the locker room, and proceeded to cut his wrists.

At that point one of the club members happened in and, not noticing Joe's desperate condition, offhandedly said, "Hey, Joe, we need a fourth for tomorrow morning—how 'bout it?"

Joe looked up and said, "What time?"

A woman goes into the pro shop at her club and reaches for an iron from a set of clubs on display. As she pulls the club from the bag she unleashes an enormous fart. Pretending nothing happened, she turns to the pro and asks, "How much are these?"

The pro responds, "Well, if you farted by simply touching them, you're going to shit when you hear the price!"

During our weekly Lamaze class, the instructor emphasized the importance of exercise, hinting strongly that husbands need to get out and start walking with their wives. From the back of the room one expectant father inquired, "Would it be okay if she carries a bag of golf clubs while she walks?"

Four gentlemen go out to play golf one sunny morning. One is detained in the clubhouse, and the other three are discussing their children while walking to the 1st tee. "My son," says one, "has made quite a name for himself in the home building industry. He began as a carpenter, but now owns his own design and construction firm. He's so successful, in fact, that in the last year he was able to give a good friend a brand-new home as a gift."

The second man, not to be outdone, allows how his son began his career as a car salesman, but now owns a multi-line dealership. "He's so successful, in fact, that in the last six months he gave a friend two brand-new cars as gifts."

The third man's son has worked his way up through a stock brokerage firm and in the last few weeks has given a good friend a large stock portfolio as a gift.

As the fourth man arrives at the 1st tee box, another tells him that they have been discussing their progeny and asks what line his son is in. "To tell the truth, I'm not very pleased with how my son has turned out," he replies. "For fifteen years, he's been a hairdresser, and I've just recently discovered he's a practicing homosexual. But, on the bright side, he must be very good at what he does because his last three boyfriends have given him a brand-new house, two cars, and a big pile of stock certificates."

Once the club duffer challenged the local golf pro to a match, with a $100 bet on the side. "But," said the duffer, "since you're obviously much better than I, to even it a bit you have to spot me two 'gotchas.'"

The golf pro didn't know what a "gotcha" was, but he went along with it. And off they went.

Coming back to the 19th hole, the rest of the club members were amazed to see the golf pro paying the duffer $100.

"What happened?" asked one of the members.

"Well," said the pro, "I was teeing up for the 1st hole, and as I brought the club down, that jerk stuck his hand between my legs and grabbed my crotch and yelled 'Gotcha!'"

"Have you ever tried to play 18 holes of golf waiting for the second 'gotcha'?"

Two longtime golfers were standing overlooking the river, getting ready to hit their shots. One golfer looked to the other and said, "Look at those idiots over there fishin' in the rain."

Q. Why are golf and sex so similar?

A. They are the two things you can thoroughly enjoy even though you are really bad at them.

Two golfers just came back to the clubhouse for a drink. They overheard two Irishmen talking. "I used to live in Dublin too," said one. "I moved here when I was ten too," said the other. "My last name is O'Leary too."

The two golfers that had heard asked a man walking by, "Who are these guys?"

The man said, "Oh! That's the O'Leary twins, they're just drunk."

Fred had tried to be particularly careful about his language as he played golf with his preacher. But on the 12th hole, when he twice failed to hit out of a sand trap, he lost his resolve and let fly with a string of expletives.

The preacher felt obliged to respond. "I have observed," said he in a calm voice, "that the best golfers do not use foul language."

"I guess not," said Fred, "but what the hell do they have to cuss about?"

A fellow goes to the doctor and says, "Doc, every time I swing my 7-iron I pass this outrageous gas."

He swings the iron in the doctor's office and breaks a loud sound of wind. He swings the 8-iron and nothing, he swings the 6 and nothing. He swings the 7 again, and again the same loud sound is heard, followed by a very foul smell.

The doctor says, "H'mm, interesting case," and gets up and grabs a long pole lying against the wall.

"What are you going to do with that?" the fellow nervously asks, fearing the worst.

"Oh, don't worry. I'm just going to open the window and let some air into this room," the doc replies.

My wife inquired as to why I don't play golf with Dean anymore. I asked her, "Would you continue to play with a guy who always gets drunk, loses so many balls that other groups are always playing through, who tells lousy jokes while you are trying to putt, and generally offends everyone around him on the course?"

"Certainly not, dear," she replied.

"Well, neither would he."

A couple whose passion had waned saw a marriage counselor and went through a number of appointments that brought little success. Suddenly at one session the counselor grabbed the wife and kissed her passionately.

"There," he said to the husband. "That's what she needs every Monday, Wednesday, Saturday, and Sunday."

"Well," replied the husband, "I can bring her in on Mondays and Wednesdays but Saturdays and Sundays are my golf days."

A foursome watches a lone player play up short of the green they are on. As they tee off at the next hole they watch the lone player quickly chip on and putt out.

He almost runs to the tee where the foursome is.

He looks at the bewildered players and says, "Would you mind if I play through? I've just heard my wife has had a terrible accident."

Golf: A game where you yell fore, you get six, and you write five.

Two Scotsmen, Sandy and Angus, are playing golf one day and come upon a water hole. Sandy hits and sends one into the middle of the pond. He reaches into his bag and finds that he has no balls remaining. He asks Angus for a ball and promptly hits that one into the pond as well. This goes on four more times and when he asks Angus for a sixth ball, Angus says, "Sandy, these balls cost me a lot of money," to which Sandy replies, "Angus, lad, if you can't afford to play the game, you should not be out here."

Standing on the tee of a relatively long par-3, the confident golfer said to his caddie, "Looks like a 4-wood and a putt to me." The caddie handed him the 4-wood, which he topped, sending the ball about 15 yards off the front of the tee.

Immediately the caddie handed him his putter and said, "And now for one hell of a putt."

A guy receives an ad in **the** mail for a golf resort where everything costs one dollar. He jumps at the offer and heads off for a weekend of fun in the sun. He arrives and plays a round of golf. **It** costs him a buck. When he goes for dinner that evening, it costs him another buck. His room is only a buck a day! The day before he's to check out, he heads out to play a last round and stops by the pro shop and charges a sleeve of three balls to his room. When he's checking out next morning, he looks at the bill and sees: Golf: $1.00, Dinner: $1.00, Room: $1.00, Sleeve of golf balls: $3,000. He hits the ceiling! Calling over to the manager, he asks, "What is this all about? Everything is supposed to cost one dollar, and you charged me $3,000 for three golf balls?" "I'm sorry, sir," said the manager, "but you didn't read the fine print in our promotional brochure. That's what our golf balls cost." "Well," said the man, "if I wanted to spend that kind of money, I could've gone to that luxury hotel across the street and paid them $1,000 a day for a room. At least I would've known what I was paying for!" "That's right, sir, you could have," said the manager. "Over there they get you by the room. Over here we get you by the balls!"

Several years ago my wife and I were giving a golf class called "Golf for Novices." It was for novice or beginner golfers to teach them the very basics of the game. It included such things as the grip, stance, and the swing. We also covered things like etiquette and what to expect when you make your first trip to a golf course. We mentioned that at our course there are two colored tees. The men play the blue tees and the women play the red tees.

A few weeks later Bill arrived home fairly late one evening from his golf game. He was living with Mary, who happened to have been one of our enthusiastic, but not too bright, students. She was somewhat agitated that he arrived home late but it wasn't until he emptied his pockets onto his dresser that she went ballistic.

She flew into an intense rage and demanded to know who the woman was that he had been golfing with. He hadn't a clue what her problem was and said he'd been playing with his pals, Brad, Jim, and Elmer. She continued her tirade and said, "Don't you lie to me. I know you were with some woman." Finally he asked her to explain where she was coming from.

She replied, "I know you were with some woman because I took that beginner golfer course. They told me women play red tees and you just put some red tees on your dresser!"

A golfer ran into an old buddy at the driving range one day. They talked about their games, their swings, and all manner of things.

Eventually, one of them said, "How's the family?"

The other replied, "Oh, pretty good. I got a new set of clubs for my wife the other day!"

"Hey, good trade!" replied the good buddy.

A man wants to play golf, but shows up at the golf course by himself. The starter groups him with three ladies, currently on the 1st hole. Upon walking up to the tee, the man sees the three ladies are nuns. He thinks to himself, "I gotta watch my p's and q's!"

Everyone introduces everyone else on the 1st tee and one of the nuns says to the man, "Go ahead, sir! You're up."

The man takes a deep breath and proceeds to tee off. The ball goes down the fairway, hits a rock, and bounces directly to the right into the sand bunker. The man says, "Jesus Christ! Did you see that?" forgetting his audience.

He is instantly embarrassed when he comes to his senses, and one of the nuns says, "We don't talk that way in the presence of the Lord. Watch your language, sir. Now step aside, it's my turn."

The nun winds up and swings as absolutely hard as she can. The ball slices almost instantly, hits a tree dead center, and bounces out of bounds across the parking lot. The nun bends over, gets her tee, and mutters "Goddamnit!" as she walks by the man.

The man, rather amused and astonished, says, "Why, sister, you just said—"

The nun interrupts and finishes, "Yeah, I know what I just said. But then **again** you didn't just hit a goddamn tree, did you?"

A man, while playing the front nine on a complicated golf course, became confused as to where he was on the course. Looking around, he saw a lady playing ahead of him. He walked up to her, explained his confusion, and asked her if she knew what hole he was playing. She replied, "I'm on the 7th hole, and you are a hole **behind** me, so you must be on **the** 6th hole." He thanked her and went back to his golf.

On the back nine the same thing happened; and he approached her again with the same request. She said, "I'm on the 14th hole, you are a hole behind me, so you must be on the 13th hole." Once again he thanked her and returned to his play.

He finished his round and went to the clubhouse, where he saw the same lady sitting at the end of the bar. He asked the bartender if he knew the lady. The bartender said that she was a saleslady and played the course often. He approached her and said, "Let me buy you a drink in appreciation for your help. I **understand** that you are in the sales profession. I'm in sales also. What do you sell?"

She replied, "If I tell you, you'll laugh."

"No, I won't."

"Well, if you must know," she answered, "I work for Tampax." With that, he laughed so hard he almost lost his breath. She said, "See I knew you would laugh."

"That's not what I'm laughing at," he replied. "I'm a salesman for Preparation H, so I'm still a hole behind you!"

A golfer had made an awful shot and tore up a large piece of turf. He picked it up and, looking about, said, "What shall I do with this?"

"If I were you," said the caddie, "I'd take it home to practice on."

An avid golfer comes home from the golf course to find his wife standing in front of a full-length mirror, taking a hard look at herself.

"You know, dear," she says. "I look in the mirror and I see an old woman. My face is all wrinkled, my boobs are barely above my waist, and my butt is hanging out a mile. I've got fat legs, and my arms are all flabby." She turns to her husband, who is practicing his putting, and says, "Tell me something positive to make me feel better about myself."

He studies hard for a moment while continuing to perfect his stroke and in a soft, thoughtful voice says, "Well, there's nothing wrong with your eyesight."

A wife walked into the bedroom and found her husband

in bed with his golf clubs. Seeing the astonished look on her face, he calmly said, "Well, you said I had to choose, right?"

If you think it's hard to meet new people, pick up the wrong golf ball on the course sometime.

Two women are playing golf, when one of them asks the other, "Do you and your husband have mutual climax?"

The other woman replies, "No, I think we have State Farm."

The golfer called one of the caddies and said, "I want a caddie who can count and keep the score. What's three and four and five add up to?"

"Eleven, sir," said the caddie.

"Good, you'll do perfectly."

The man who invented golf and said it was "fun" is the same guy that invented bagpipes and said it was "music."

Golfer: "Would you mind wading into the pond and retrieving my ball?"

Caddie: "Why?"

Golfer: "It's my lucky ball."

A man was invited to play at his friend's course and during the round he felt the call of nature. He was too far away from the toilets and so he went behind a tree, believing that he was unobserved.

However, on a parallel fairway, three lady members were playing. As they passed they were surprised to observe just a very private part of a man's anatomy protruding from around the tree.

"He's certainly not my husband, I can tell you that," said the first lady.

"Disgusting! I'm glad he's not mine either," said the second lady.

"It really is an outrage," said the third. "He's not even a club member!"

New Rules for 2006

There are many rules that have become customary behavior and we're not sure whether they are rules or folklore. But since we are irreverent types, we need to take a look at some things we think need to change. So for now, a little venting. We are all speaking now. We have the mouth.

This is a long P.S. but we'll put it in here to get your juices flowing. Golf is considered to be a gentleman's game and a game where one's honor is relied upon to enforce the rules. The simple task of counting up one's strokes on each hole can put enormous pressure on one's psyche and self-esteem. No one really wants to record a snowman (8) or a melting snowman (10) or a snowball from hell (12) on his or her scorecard. But the ethics of the game require it. No other game reminds us so often just what a bunch of insecure liars we all really are. We all want a lower handicap, but when we finally get one, we want a higher one. So before we get into the rules we should change, don't complicate this book by not recording your scores properly. It will prove to be the basis for your own self-improvement.

Now for those rules that don't make any sense and need to be changed.

1. Ball in a divot **in** the middle of a fairway. What's the deal with this? The odds of getting a hole in one are one in a million or more and we constantly hit the ball and have it land in someone else's diggings. Repairing them is the golf course maintenance crew's responsibility. If the guy before us had a chance to make his own fresh divot, so should we. Move the ball. No penalty.

2. Ball in a footprint in a sand trap. For cry eye! We see no good reason to be forced to play a shot from a heel print because some dumb jerk ahead of us didn't rake the trap. Take a drop and if you see him, penalize him three shots.

3. Ball along a fence marking out of bounds. Hey, if the golf course you are playing can't afford to own the real estate surrounding the course, don't take it out on us. We are entitled to a free and clear swing anywhere on the course where a man-made obstruction interferes with our swings. Take a drop and have a good hack.

4. Greenside sprinkler head is in line with my putt from off the green. Don't tell me to play a wedge and go over the sprinkler. We are entitled to play the club we want under normal conditions. Move the ball or, better yet, dig up the sprinkler head. That pile of dirt is certainly in your way now.

5. Now, here's an etiquette rule that needs a change. Play-

ers on opposite sides of the fairway need to hit the ball. Don't be standing there looking at each other to determine who is away. Hit the damn ball. There are people who are away from their families out here who want to get home.

6. The same rule applies on the green. Putt when you are ready. You can always line it up later.

7. Oh yes. Teeing off. The first guy to the tee . . . hits. End of story.

8. Out of bounds. This rule needs some thought. Stroke and distance is just a little too severe. Cripes, I just hit my Pro V1 where it is unretrievable. That's four bucks down the drain. Isn't that enough? This game will bleed us to death if we aren't careful.

9. If you have the strength to walk the course and the willingness to spend the money for a caddie, you are entitled to some benefit, so we would allow the caddie to improve your lie anytime he wants to, provided this takes place well before you arrive at the ball and provided he doesn't place it on a tee. (We would require some creativity from the caddie.)

10. It's not easy to hit a great putt, so when you hit one that just lips out here's our suggestion: Any putt hitting the cup or pin that comes to rest within four inches of the cup shall be counted as a made putt with no stroke added for the tap-in. This is also true for putts coming to rest on the lip.

Conclusion

We thought about looking at golf as a metaphor for life. For some it may be, but for us, whether it's golf or life, hopefully the message is apparent: Savor the moment, have a chuckle or two, and keep looking for the hidden secrets that make golf and life more enjoyable.

Code Template

L_ _ _n f_ _ _ y_ _ _ m_ _ _ _ _ _s a_ _ t_ _
n_ _ to m_ _ _ t_ _ s_ _ _ m_ _ _ _ _ _
t_ _ _e. S_ _ _ in t_ _ m_ _ _n a_ _
c_ _c_ _t_ _t_ o_ wh_ _ y_ _ w_ _ _ t_
ac_ _ _ _p_ _ _h w_ _ _ a s_ _t b_ _ _ _e
y_ _ h_ _ it. D_ _'_ b_ t_ _ _ _ _ng o_
h_ _ ex_ _ _ _ _g it w_ _ _ _ b_ to win
y_ _ _ m_ _ _ _ o_ h_ _ m_ _ _ t_ _ub_ _ y_ _
c_ _ _ _ g_ i_ i_ y_ _ m_ _ _ t_ _ s_ _ _.
E_ _ _ _ _ _ _e t_ _ _ _ _ _ b_
s_ _ _ _ _ _g the c_ _ _ w_ _ _ f_ _ _ _ _ _ _ and
rh_ _ _ _. Pr_ _ _ _ _e y_ _ _ w_ _ _n_ _ _s a_ _
u_ _ _ _ _ _ _ _d y_ _ _ st_ _ _ _ _ _ _. But
r_ _em_ _r, w_ _ _ _h_ _ _ s_ _ _ _s
h_ _ _ n_v_ _ b_ _ _ g_v_ _ f_ _ $15 US/$20
Canadian.

But if you really want to lower your scores here is the secret Angus shared only with his friends:

The earth is roughly 25,000 miles around at the equator. Once a day it travels completely around its axis so if you are not a mathematician, it is spinning at about 1,000 miles per hour. The earth is roughly 93,000,000 miles from the sun. Using the formula for circumference (Pi times 2[radius]) we can estimate the orbit of the earth around the sun to be approximately 585,000,000 miles. Since the earth circles the sun once a year, it travels 1,600,000 miles every day, or 66,000 miles per hour. With all that high-speed spinning and traveling we're lucky to stand up, let alone make a three-foot putt.

S_, w___ f__e_ w___ a s____ p__t, m___
y___ b__l and c____ i_. R_pl__ t__
b___ and r_____ t__ mark. N_w t___
y___ p__t__ a__ sl____ t___ fo__
p_____ce s____s. Li__ i_ up a____.
K____ b_h_n_ t__ b___. S__nd u_
sl____. F____ly a__r___ the b___. W___
y__ h__e d___ a__ th__, st___
s____ly i__o the e__s o_ t__ o____
pl____s and j___ w___ un___ y__
h__ t____ w____: "T___'s g___.
P___ i_ u_."

Code Solution

ANSWER KEY

Learn from your mistakes and try not to make the same mistake twice. Stay in the moment and concentrate on what you want to accomplish with a shot before you hit it. Don't be thinking of how exciting it would be to win your match or how much trouble you could get in if you miss the shot. Eliminate tension by swinging the club with fluidity and rhythm. Practice your weaknesses and understand your strengths. But remember, worthwhile secrets have never been given for $15 US/$20 Canadian.

The secret Angus shared only with his friends: So, when faced with a short putt, mark your ball and clean it. Replace the ball and remove the mark. Now take your putter and slowly take four practice swings. Line it up again. Kneel behind the ball. Stand up slowly. Finally, address the ball. When you have done all that, stare somberly into the eyes of the other players and just wait until you hear these words: "That's good. Pick it up."

About the Authors

Bob Gilhooley

An avid golfer who is known as a student of the game, Bob was inspired to study the art of hitting the second shot first after he completed the amazing feat of 3-putting every hole on his home course. He accomplished this in only five rounds. Unable to rest on his laurels, Gilhooley traveled to Arizona and, remarkably, did the same thing in just three rounds.

Like Tiger Woods, Bob was trained by his father, who at one time had seventeen successive nines but missed a two-foot tap-in on 18 to ruin a perfect round. His dad passed along the secrets of course management which Bob still uses today.

Gilhooley has a master's degree in biomolecular physics from the University of Michigan. After spending a year in New Zealand, he wrote his thesis on the difference in the gravitational effects on a golf ball between the southern and northern hemispheres. He holds several patents on a variety of devices designed to improve one's golf scores, the most popular being, yes, the eraser.

Bob is married with three children and is the proud grandpa of triplets. These days, Bob spends his free time 3-putting greens all across the country.

Jim Bronner

On Jim Bronner's sixty-second birthday, three golfers, a golf journalist, and a golf architect were inducted into the World Golf Hall of Fame. As luck would have it, the Golf Hall of Fame afforded the co-author absolutely no consideration whatsoever as an inductee. Bronner had to settle for a quiet day with his wife of thirty-seven years, Barbara, in their home in Highland Park, Illinois, and telephone calls from his two adult children, Jamie Chomas and Michael Bronner.

For the past fifty-two years Bronner has been trying to learn the secret of hitting his second shots first. Of course, had he not been such a slow learner, he might be joining that Hall of Fame class as an inductee for any one of his several major championships. However, without those championships, he has been relegated for nearly thirty years, along with his co-author, to the more modest pursuit of representing professional baseball players and having to listen to those so-called athletes explain that hitting a baseball moving at ninety miles per hour (plus) is more difficult than hitting a stationary golf ball on a tee.

All that being said, Bronner hopes that with the publication of this powerful secret code, and the certain and immediate influence it will have on improving the game of millions of golfers everywhere, he and Gilhooley can now sit confidently by their respective telephones waiting for the Golf Hall of Fame's call.